My World

Edited by Shelagh Brown

The Reverend Shelagh Brown is a writer, a broadcaster, and Editor of BRF's *New Daylight* Notes which start in January 1989. She has worked in commuterland and the inner city and is now Director of the Archbishop Coggan Training and Service Centre and Honorary Deacon at Southwark Cathedral. Her books include *Someone There — Making sense of Christianity* (SCM); *Drawing Near to the City — Christians speak about Dying* and *Married to the Church* (ed.) (SPCK); *Lent for Busy People* (BRF), best-selling Lent book for 1987; and *The Art of being a Single Woman* (Kingsway 1989). She has done 'Thought for the Day' and 'Prayer for the Day' on Radio 4, some of which appear in this book on Sundays and reveal her own understanding of people and theology.

- The Bible Reading Fellowship was founded 'to encourage the systematic and intelligent reading of the Bible, to emphasize its spiritual message and to take advantage of new light shed on Holy Scripture'.
- Over the years the Fellowship has proved a trustworthy guide for those who want an open, informed and contemporary approach to the Bible. It retains a sense of the unique authority of Scripture as a prime means by which God communicates.
- As an ecumenical organization, the Fellowship embraces all Christian traditions and its readers are to be found in most parts of the world.

My World

Edited by
Shelagh Brown

the bible reading fellowship

The Bible Reading Fellowship
Warwick House
25 Buckingham Palace Road
London SW1W 0PP

First published 1989

British Library CIP data

My World
1. Christian Life — Prayers & readings
I. Brown, Shelagh
242'.8

ISBN 0-900164-77-8

Printed by Bocardo Press Ltd, Didcot.

CONTENTS

Acknowledgements

Bible quotations are mostly taken from the Revised Standard Version, copyright 1973 by Division of Christian Education of the National Council of the Churches of Christ in the USA.

Other versions indicated:

NEB New English Bible: Oxford and Cambridge University Presses 1970;
GNB Good News Bible (Today's English Version): American Bible Society 1976
JB Jerusalem Bible: Darton, Longman & Todd Ltd and Doubleday & Co. Inc. 1968;
NJB New Jerusalem Bible: Darton, Longman & Todd Ltd and Doubleday & Co. Inc. 1985.

The following quotations and prayers are copyright and are included by kind permission of the copyright holders.

'A Prayer for Reconciliation' in *Prayers from Taizé*, reprinted by permission of A. R. Mowbray and Company Ltd.

'Father, Forgive' reprinted by permission of Coventry Cathedral.

Extract from *Towards the Recovery of a Lost Bequest*, by Roger Dowley, reprinted by permission of Scripture Union.

Extract from *The Prophet* by Kahlil Gibran reprinted by permission of William Heinemann Ltd.

Extract from *Under the Eye of the Clock* by Christopher Nolan, published by Weidenfeld & Nicolson, 1988, is used by permission of the publishers.

Extract from *Praying the Kingdom* by Charles Elliott, published and copyright 1985 by Darton, Longman & Todd, Ltd., reprinted by permission of the publishers.

Material from *The Alternative Service Book 1980* is copyright and reproduced by kind permission of the Central Board of Finance of the Church of England.

ADDRESSES

Greenpeace, 30–31 Islington Green, London N1 8BR

International Fund for Animal Welfare, Tubwell House, New Road, Crowborough, East Sussex, TN6 2QH.

WWF (World Wildlife Fund), Panda House, Weyside Park, Godalming, Surrey, GU7 1XR.

Friends of the Earth, 377 City Road, London EC1V 1NA

PREFACE

It's My World Too. . .!

A few weeks ago I noticed a baby seal printed on the front of a woman's T-shirt. It was the logo of the International Fund for Animal Welfare, and it had some words underneath:

It's my world too. . .

That phrase says just why I have called this book *My World*. 'Wouldn't it be better to call it *Your World*?' said some people. Others suggested *Our World*. But when something is mine then I am in a special relationship with it and I have a special claim upon it.

When I say that my dark green MGB is '*my* car' that feels (and is) totally different from saying that it is '*your* car' or '*our* car', and because it really is my car then you will (dare I say 'ought to'?) have a different attitude to it.

I may be delighted for you to share it. But if you assume that you can drive my car whenever and however you like, or if you put sand in the engine so that it cannot run smoothly, or take it away from me so that I cannot use it at all, then I shall be more likely to see you as my enemy than my friend. That is not to say I won't come round to praying for you, since Jesus said that was what we were to do to our enemies, and I shall struggle and pray until I can get to the point of obedience. But my first, natural reaction will be to resent you and feel very angry.

So if we can hear the baby seal and all other animal and human creatures saying to us 'It's my world too. . .', that might help us to admit their right to it. Once we have admitted it we shall know that if we take it away from them then the human creatures amongst them will probably be resentful and angry.

What would you feel like if someone took away your car or your home or the land that you live in? Or if you had to watch your children dying of hunger while half the world was stuffing itself with too much food and drink and seriously overweight (not to mention the millions of pounds and dollars it spent on feeding its dogs and cats)?

I wanted to start this book with the baby seal and the poor, the oppressed and the hungry as they cry out to us 'It's my world too. . .' But I want us to end up with an even deeper realization of the truth that we all know, that ultimately it is only God who can say 'It's my world'. A song by the Fisher Folk puts that truth beautifully and biblically into words.

I walk with you my children, through valleys filled with gloom;
In echoes of the starlight, and shadows of the moon,
In the whispers of the night wind are gentle words for you
To touch you and assure you it's my world you're walking through.

It is God's world that we are walking through. But it is a troubled world which is in a lot of pain, and many of us would like it to be healed. The prayer of Teresa of Avila says that for that to happen Christ needs our help.

Christ has no body now on earth but yours;
yours are the only hands with which he can do his work,
yours are the only feet with which he can go about the world,
yours are the only eyes through which his compassion
can shine forth upon a troubled world.
Christ has no body now on earth but yours.

We look helplessly at the problems of the inner city, the third world, the ghettoes of race and unemployment, and forests that are dying from acid rain. We don't know what on earth to do, and we are like the disciples who looked helplessly at 5,000 hungry people. 'There is a boy here with five loaves and two small fishes,' they said to Jesus, 'but what are they among so many?' Yet the disciples discovered what can happen when even tiny resources are put into the hands of Jesus.

My World is an action book for Christians, so I have interviewed people who are supremely competent to talk about the needs of the world that God loves and wants us to love and care for and pray for. In *Lent for Busy People* the contributors chose a passage from the Bible and then commented on it. In *My World* I have (almost always) started with what people said, and then chosen a relevant Bible pasages to set alongside their words.

From Monday to Saturday there is an interview and a Bible reading for each day, and also a meditation or a prayer. Some of the prayers are by the contributors, some (marked with asterisks) are by me, and some are the famous and much loved prayers of the saints through the centuries.

Sundays are different, and I have done two things. First there is an introduction to the theme for the week, and then there is something based on various Prayers for the Day which I gave on BBC Radio 4 (though the two on John were not broadcast; they were in an alternative series, which was just as suitable. But the producer and I finally chose the talks on Isaiah).

There is a weekly outline for a study group, with questions for discussion and a suggestion for a meditation. This is printed in a box within the week and covers its theme.

My World is the BRF's Advent book for 1988, but it is suitable for individuals and groups to use at any time of the year (including Lent). There are six weeks altogether, and if you are using it for Advent 1988 then there is a Christmas reading for the 25th December. But just as the Easter message of forgiveness, death and resurrection is a continual and integral part of the Christian life, so is the Christmas message of peace on earth and the wonder of the fact that 'the Word became flesh and dwelt among us'.

Perhaps, as well as the daily prayers that go with the daily readings in *My World*, you might like every day to pray the Coventry Cathedral Prayer which is carved on a plaque in the ruins. The cathedral is a sign and a symbol of reconciliation between people who were once enemies.

Father, Forgive. . .

The hatred which divides nation from nation,
  race from race, class from class,
Father, forgive.
The covetous desires of men and nations
  to possess what is not their own,
Father, forgive.
The greed which exploits the labours of men,
  and lays waste the earth,
Father, forgive.
Our envy of the welfare and happiness of others,
Father, forgive.
Our indifference to the plight of the homeless
  and the refugee,
Father, forgive.
The lust which uses for ignoble ends
  the bodies of men and women,
Father, forgive.
The pride which leads to trust in ourselves
  and not in God,
Father, forgive.

Copies of this prayer (in English, French, German and Spanish) are available from Coventry Cathedral, CV1 5ES; send s.a.e. plus a 19p stamp.

Week 1

THE INNER CITY

THE BIBLE SAYS that heaven is going to be like a city. In his vision on the Isle of Patmos St John sees a new heaven and a new earth, and the holy city coming down out of heaven from God, prepared as a bride adorned for her husband. It's a strange mixing of metaphors, but the city speaks of people living together in one place, and a wedding speaks of loving in the deepest and most intimate way that it is possible to love.

Inside the city there is a garden, with the tree of life growing there, and the river of the water of life, bright as crystal, flowing from the throne of God through the middle of the street of the city. The servants of God will worship him there, it says, and they shall see his face: and 'night shall be no more; they will need no light of lamp or sun, for the Lord God will be their light, and they shall reign for ever and ever'.

Our cities are not like the city of God. Instead of walking along streets that are bright with the love of God we walk along streets that are full of fear and darkness. Women are raped. Old people are mugged. Angry, resentful people with no hope strike out blindly in vandalism and violence. Sinful cities. But also unhappy, unblessed cities, and it is the will of God that they should be happy and blessed. Under God it is the task of the people of God to make them so.

BREAD FOR THE WORLD

It was near the time of Passover, the great Jewish festival. Raising his eyes and seeing a large crowd coming towards him, Jesus said to Philip, 'Where are we to buy bread to feed these people?' This he said to test him; Jesus himself knew what he meant to do.

Philip replied, 'Twenty pounds would not buy enough bread for every one of them to have a little.' One of his disciples, Andrew, the brother of Simon Peter, said to him, 'There is a boy here who has five barley loaves and two fishes; but what is that among so many?'

Jesus said, 'Make the people sit down.' There was plenty of grass there, so the men sat down, about five thousand of them. Then Jesus took the loaves, gave thanks and distributed them to the people as they sat there. He did the same with the fishes, and they had as much as they wanted. . .

(John 6:4–11 NEB)

Two small fishes and five small barley loaves — and they were going to be the boy's meal. It doesn't say why he had something and nobody else did, but that doesn't seem to be the point of the story. The point was that there were a lot of hungry people who didn't have any food.

These people weren't starving, but always when I read this it makes me think of the pictures we see on television. Little children standing in a line, with arms and legs that are so thin you'd think they'd snap. . . and pot bellies sticking out and great big eyes looking at the camera out of sad faces. Faces that don't seem to have any hope in them — and the whole situation feels hopeless. There are so many of them that we can't think what to do.

Five barley loaves and two small fishes — and what use are they going to be when we look at the size of the problem? But the boy who had the loaves and the fishes handed them over. It doesn't say whether he handed them over to Andrew or to Jesus — but they ended up in the hands of Jesus, and the five thousand people ended up getting fed. Because the boy gave what he had. . .

All that happened a long time ago. But there's a modern day equivalent of the boy. A scruffy looking candidate for the Nobel Peace Prize, with untidy hair and jeans — and his last record was Bread for the World, two years after he'd launched Band Aid.

Band Aid happened because Bob Geldorf gave what he had got for the starving. He hadn't got the greatest voice in the world, but it had got him into the charts. And because of the Band Aid concerts a little bit more of the world started to get fed. . .

In a school where I was doing the morning assembly there were Band Aid sacks and the children would come up after their last hymn with things to put into the sacks. One sack labelled BEANS, another sack labelled SUGAR and another sack labelled FLOUR. . . A small girl would put in a bag of beans, and a small boy a bag of sugar, and another one a bag of flour — and then we're back to the boy with five barley loaves and the two small fishes. And what were they among so many? But he gave them, and it says that Jesus himself knew what he meant to do. . .

A PRAYER Lord, there are so many hungry people in the world that we don't know what to do. Show us what we can give you — so that there can be bread for the world.

Bishop David Sheppard 1/Monday

THE CENTRE OF THE UNIVERSE!

On the train to Liverpool, where I was to interview David Sheppard, I got into conversation with three young men: George Rix, David Windsor and Christopher Jones. When I told them about this book they agreed to answer some questions for me and let me record them.

So tell me what you're doing. I'm coming home for a couple of days.
Why are you going to London? I'm working there.
Why aren't you working in Liverpool? Expansion!
How many times do you go down? Three times a week. I've got a wife. I only use Liverpool people, so they're commuting up and down as well.
What do you think of Liverpool? Liverpool is the centre of the universe!
So what needs doing to it? It needs more money, more jobs.
Anything else? Not really. The people would do the rest.
What's it like living in Liverpool? Bad news. No work. No nothing.

What are you doing up in London? Looking for work.
Have you got any work? No.
What would you like doing in Liverpool? Building factories. More work. More education for the kids.
You said it was suicidal here. Tell me about that boy you knew. Oh, he was only 19, and he threw himself off the heights. Very depressed. It's not the first time. There was a couple that fell over there. Threw themselves off, like. . .depressed.
So it's money? It's work? Just work. That's all I can say. Goodbye.

I started off my interview with David Sheppard by telling him about

these men, and he said that there were hundreds of others like them. He has met them.

I often go to London on Fridays, and the 18.20 from London is a piece of history. It is crowded with people like that. There are so many of them that they always have to run a back-up train, and both of them will go out packed to the doors. It is a dramatic form of something that has gone on for 150 years in every big city.

We have allowed there to be an assumption in education (even in Christian education). The assumption is that if people do well they will go up in the world, and they will move away. Your philosophy and your beliefs are geared to the idea that if people are worthy and hard-working they will make it — and move away.

What that actually does to the communities they leave behind is obvious. If in every generation the people with self-confidence all go away the task of those who stay behind becomes that much harder each time round.

As Christians I believe we have got to do two things. We have got to see the human potential and the God-given gifts which are there within every community. But we have also got to address some of the public issues (which does mean political issues), which will produce a good mixture of decent housing, a good mixture of jobs and a good mixture of decent schools in each of these communities. We mustn't connive at an increasingly segregated and divided society. The bigger the city the bigger the divisions are.

Merseyside was once a great port. All the trade of the Midlands and the North went through it to North America and the Empire. But now its original

Bishop David Sheppard

David Sheppard is married to Grace, and they have a daughter, Jenny. He played cricket for England and experienced a personal conversion to Christ whilst at Cambridge after a nominal Christian upbringing. He met inner-city life following ordination, first in Islington, then in Canning Town. He likes reading, music, painting, the theatre and being with his family. Books: *Parson's Pitch; Built as a City; Bias to the Poor* and (jointly with Archbishop Derek Worlock) *Better Together*.

purpose is no longer there. Once it filled a great need for this country — but now it isn't needed any more. That is a national issue.

When I served on the Archbishop of Canterbury's Commission on Urban Priority areas we often found ourselves, as we went around the country, using those words of St Paul: 'We are members one of another. . .' We realized that we were not just looking at urban priority areas. We were looking at the whole nation.

* * *

For just as the body is one and has many members, and all the members of the body, though many, are one body, so it is with Christ. For by one Spirit we were all baptized into one body — Jews and Greeks, slaves or free — and all were made to drink of one Spirit. For the body does not consist of one member but of many. If the foot should say, 'Because I am not a hand, I do not belong to the body,' that would not make it any less a part of the body. . . The eye cannot say to the hand, 'I have no need of you', nor again the head to the feet, 'I have no need of you.' On the contrary, the parts of the body which seem to be weaker are indispensable, and those parts of the body which we think less honourable we invest with the greater honour. . . If one member suffers, all suffer together. . . (1 Corinthians 12:12–26)

CONSIDER 'No man is an Island, entire of itself; every man is a piece of the Continent, a part of the main; if a clod be washed away by the sea, Europe is the less, as well as if a promontory were, as well as if a manor of thy friends or of thine own were; any man's death diminishes me, because I am involved in Mankind. And therefore never send to know for whom the bell tolls; It tolls for thee.'

John Donne

Bishop David Sheppard 1/Tuesday

LIVERPOOL — 2

I wasn't sure that the Archbishop's Commission on Urban Priority Areas were right to take St Paul's words about the body and apply them to a nation. Paul was talking about Christians being the body of Christ. I put that point to David Sheppard.

I would agree that St Paul meant that. But he was actually using a concept of the body older than him. The Romans talked about the body politic in the same way.

A way to understand what I am talking about is to look at what Jesus meant by the kingdom of God. There is no way of understanding that unless we pick it up in the Old Testament and discover God's concern for a kingdom of justice, and a king who would reign in justice.

God had a particular concern for those who found themselves excluded from the good opportunities, and we can see the righteousness of God toppling over in favour of those who are disadvantaged. The New Jerusalem Bible really gets it right, and wherever the word *tsedeq* comes in the prophets it is translated 'saving justice'. That is the correct translation.

Old Testament commentators say that this word moves in its meaning as it comes through the prophets. In its earliest use it meant even-handed justice. But then it means a righteousness of a particular kind which topples over in favour of those who are in dire need. It is about salvation. In other words, the righteous God is active, and intervenes in the whole world and not just in the church.

STUDY GROUP MATERIAL

The Inner City

Begin by being still for two or three minutes. Then let the leader read out the sentences in the Coventry Cathedral Prayer on page 11, with everyone else praying 'Father, forgive. . .' after each one.

1. When you look at the size of the problem, what does it make you feel? Spend some time getting in touch with your feelings — and perhaps let someone make a list of all the emotions you express.

2. Read out Jeremiah 29:4–7 on page 19, and also what David Sheppard says in the next three paragraphs. Read out what Ronald Bowlby says about the homeless on page 28. What action might you take? Perhaps do a brainstorming in which everyone makes whatever suggestion comes into their head. Write them down, and then decide which ones you can act upon.

MEDITATION AND PRAYER Do the imaginative meditation at the end of Brian Branche's piece. One person can read it out slowly, while the rest do their imagining. . .

Then be quiet for a few minutes more, and finish by reading out the prayer by Brother Roger and Mother Teresa of Calcutta on page 24.

I am convinced that the teaching of Jesus about the kingdom of God is not just about the church. It is a promise and a dream about the whole wide world. I believe that promise will only be fulfilled totally in another world by God's action, but the more seriously I take the promise of the kingdom of God — the city of God as God really wants it to be — then the more indignant I am when I see it contradicted, and the more I must do what I can to bring about change so far as it is within my power.

The kingdom of God is right at the heart of Jesus' teaching. It is a very unwestern idea and it is elusive. Elusive because it's just around the corner. It is at hand. It is going to come like a thief in the night, and you've got to be ready. It will come in power in the last day — beyond this world. It is among you, and you must recognize it.

There is a whole series of stories and actions which say what the kingdom of God is like. They show God's concern for the whole world, including the poor, the lame, the halt, the blind, and the people who got left out and the people of other races. The notion that God is concerned for the welfare of the church, but has no concern for the welfare of the city or the nation or the world into which he has put us, is totally to misunderstand the creator God, who is the God of the whole earth.

It is very striking what God says to the Jewish exiles in Babylon. In Jeremiah you can feel their shudder of horror when they realize that this is a city of evil. But Jeremiah sends them a letter:

> 'Thus says the Lord of hosts, the God of Israel, to all the exiles whom I have sent into exile from Jerusalem to Babylon: Build houses and live in them; plant gardens and eat their produce. Take wives and have sons and daughters; take wives for your sons, and give your daughters in marriage, that they may bear sons and daughters; multiply there, and do not decrease. But seek the welfare of the city where I have sent you into exile, and pray to the Lord on its behalf, for in its welfare you will find your welfare.'
>
> (Jeremiah 29:4–7)

If you want to do something about all this you have got to be willing to commit yourself to some quite hard thinking. You will have to study to understand, and then see how you can join hands with other people. I think all big cities tell us that God deliberately made the world corporate, not just a chain of individuals, and I can only bring about change if I join hands with other people.

Those people will be other Christians of all denominations. The Christian lobby is much more powerful than we think. We saw a very powerful government made to change its mind over the Sunday Trading Bill because the Christian lobby mobilized itself. I was very glad to be part of that lobby, because I care about Sunday being a different day. But I have to ask if that is actually the most important single issue in the world for the church to mobilize over. What if we really cared about overseas aid, and overseas trade and the right conditions? What if we really cared about the levels of subsistence and the levels of benefit, and the assumptions that if people are unemployed they should somehow be pushed until they get themselves employed, regardless of how huge the unemployment list might be in their area?

If the Christian lobby really cared enough about those things and mobilized itself then it would have the power to shift things in a country like this. But we don't care enough about them.

A PRAYER O God, the father of the forsaken, the help of the weak, the supplier of the needy; you teach us that love towards the race of man is the bond of perfectness, and the imitation of your blessed self. Open and touch our hearts that we may see and do, both for this world and that which is to come, the things that belong to our peace. Strengthen us in the work which we have undertaken; give us wisdom, perseverance, faith, and zeal, and in your own time and according to your pleasure prosper the issue; for the love of your Son Jesus Christ. (Anthony Ashley Cooper, Earl of Shaftesbury)

Lord Scarman 1/Wednesday

BRIXTON

Brixton was once a very pleasant, lively suburb. The people who lived there were bright and prosperous and they were the natural leaders of society. But they left. They deserted Brixton — if you give 'desert' its meaning of 'depart from'. The people who have come into this deserted area now are people who are too poor to go anywhere else.

Brixton is a place full of sad buildings. The houses, the shops and the industrial buildings are all in a state of decline. Business has left the inner city and industry has left it. Until recently the opportunities for improving one's quality of lifestyle were very few indeed. I can imagine the deep sense of frustration and deprivation that people feel. They have got problems themselves, and as well as having to live with those they are forced to live in areas of decay.

Many of the sad figures of the inner city have found it very difficult to build up self-respect. Those who once had it have found it diminished. There is just one word that sums it all up. Poverty.

But you don't relieve poverty by throwing pennies on the pavement and giving away money indiscriminately. What you've got to do is to help the people who live there to work and to fight their way out of poverty. This is extremely difficult. But the Prince of Wales has got the correct answer in principle. You help them to help themselves. Community self-help is an enormously important instrument because if it succeeds then it induces self-respect.

One important thing that has to be done is to make an onslaught on the buildings of the inner city. The built environment is unrepaired and partially destroyed. But attempts are being made and the onslaught is showing results. This week I was down in the Rotherhithe area of London and what was going on to improve the built environment was remarkable.

One value of improving the physical environment is that it will encourage people to move back there again. A danger of the inner city is that it is just the home of those who feel themselves inadequate. The people who feel themselves able to accept the challenges of our society have been moving out, and they have got to start moving in again.

In a small way the tide has turned and there is the beginning of a flow back. We mustn't reject the arrival in the inner city of the so-called Yuppies. Let them come. They have energy and intelligence and that can do an immense amount of good.

What they mustn't do is to take it over and turn it into a middle class suburb. There has got to be a diversified society of all classes. That is not a

The Right Hon. Lord Scarman

Leslie Scarman is a Lord of Appeal in Ordinary. He is married to Ruth, and they have a son. After the Brixton riots in 1981 he chaired the enquiry which looked into relationships between the police and the people who live in Brixton, and he wrote the Brixton Report. He is deeply concerned and active in inner-city issues. He has written *The Pattern of Law Reform* and *English Law — The New Dimension.* He likes gardening and walking.

word I like, but it says what I mean. There have got to be all classes there, working together and rubbing shoulders together, and each one helping the other.

The less intellectually endowed could do an enormous amount of work. They could be craftsmen and manual workers, full of self-respect, helping the so-called Yuppies. And the Yuppies could do an enormous amount in offering leadership and helping the community in that way. What I want to see is a living community embracing all classes, who all live and if possible work in the inner city. Then the place would come alive again and it would no longer be a dead end.

The inner city has lost the character of the city. When a city has 'city life' in the fullest meaning of that term (in the Greek sense), all strands of society live and work together. There is no single way to bring that about. It is a complex business. You create businesses. You establish educational institutions.

When people are rubbing shoulders together they forget racial or group prejudices. They look on each person that they meet as an individual, irrespective of the colour of his skin or his intellectual attainments, or her sex or her religion or anything else. They are assessed for their value as individuals. As soon as that happens the place gets alive.

* * *

And I saw no temple in the city, for its temple is the Lord God the Almighty and the Lamb. And the city has no need of sun or moon to shine upon it, for the glory of God is its light, and its lamp is the Lamb. By its light shall the nations walk; and the kings of the earth shall bring their glory into it, and its gates shall never be shut by day — and there shall be no night there; they shall bring into it the glory and the honour of the nations. But nothing unclean shall enter it, nor any one who practises abomination or falsehood, but only those who are written in the Lamb's book of life. Then he showed me the river of the water of life, bright as crystal, flowing from the throne of God and of the Lamb through the middle of the street of the city; also, on either side of the river, the tree of life with its twelve kinds of fruit, yielding its fruit each month; and the leaves of the tree were for the healing of the nations.

(Revelation 21:22–22:2)

A PRAYER* Lord God, you say that heaven will be a city, and that the water of the river of life will flow through the city for the healing of the nations. Please let that river flow here on earth for the healing of our cities — and show us what to do to channel it.

Archbishop Derek Worlock

Derek Worlock is the Archbishop of Liverpool and from 1953–65 he was Domestic Prelate of the Pope. He and David Sheppard, the Anglican Bishop of Liverpool, work closely together and have just written *Better Together*. Archbishop Worlock has also written *Turn and Turn Again* and *Give Me Your Hand* and compiled an anthology called *Take One at Bedtime.*

Archbishop Derek Worlock 1/Thursday

POVERTY AND THE POOR

Interest in the inner cities has now become all the vogue. Sometimes I wonder which is the greatest danger: that these grave social problems may become a party political football, kicked around for the prestige and advantage of the kicker, or that people may almost romanticize about conditions in urban priority areas (for the problems are often worse in the perimeter estates than in the actual centre of cities) and seem almost to glamourize and give an aura of holiness to situations which are at best deprivation.

People are apt to confuse poverty with the poor. The Lord said, 'Blessed are the poor,' not blessed is poverty. I suppose that poverty can be a blessed thing if freely embraced as a means of self-denial and even mortification. But poverty, enforced poverty, often speaks of injustice: something to be eradicated, not beatified.

God so loved the world that he sent his beloved Son as a redeemer and to show us how to live in it. Religion has constantly upheld the virtue of simplicity. But nowhere did Jesus do other than condemn those who wrought injustice or closed their eyes to its victims.

Bad housing, long-term unemployment, lack of job opportunity, all these things are aspects of poverty and injustice. Sometimes I hear people vying with one another at conferences and debates as to who has got it worst. The northerner speaks of the soul-destroying nature of long-term unemployment. The southerner speaks of the threat to stability in the home and family which can be caused by acute anxiety and possible future redundancy.

What, then, is poverty — in inner cities or any other area of deprivation for that matter? I once heard two priests discussing this question, high up in the Andes where they were endeavouring to serve scattered communities, for the most part Peruvian Indians. They reached an intriguing conclusion: 'Poverty is the absence of access to outside stimulus.'

I asked for examples and they spoke of conditions where there was no radio or television, no capacity to read even if a newspaper were to be had in the area. There was no means of letting them know of standards and a quality of life which might encourage them to try to better their own living. Not that they were happy to be free of such outside pressures. The squalor of much of their lives prevented that. There was nothing to push them to try to improve their lot. 'These people do not even know they are poor,' said the priest. 'They do not even know that they live in Peru. They just exist, sheltering in a hut or lean-to if the weather is bad: just existing, waiting for the next birth, the next death.'

Because of the dignity of God's creation, the priest was working with the men of the area to build a road out of the valley. The other had arranged for a local man to learn how to inseminate the local herd of cattle with a new, strong strain from North America, to increase the size of the calves and the eventual milk yield.

The same principle applies to urban priority areas in our own country, rapidly shut in upon themselves through lack of job opportunity and of outside investment needed to improve their living conditions. Priests who work with the people to alleviate such conditions are not trouble-makers. Hopelessness is at the heart of poverty and good news needs to be given practical form, even if at times it leads to the charge of religion interfering with politics.

Isaiah 61, which speaks of the Lord sending his prophets to bring the good news to the poor, also (vv. 5–6) says,

> Strangers will come forward to feed your flocks, foreigners be your ploughmen and vinedressers, and you will be called priests of the Lord and be addressed as ministers of God.

A PRAYER

O God the Father of all,
you ask every one of us to spread
love where the poor are humiliated,
joy where the church is brought low,

and reconciliation where people are divided
father against son, mother against daughter,
husband against wife,
believers against those who cannot believe,
Christians against their unloved fellow Christians.
You open this way for us,
so that the wounded body of Jesus Christ, your church,
may be leaven of communion for the poor of the earth
and in the whole human family.

(Brother Roger & Mother Teresa of Calcutta)

The Revd Brian Branche — 1/Friday

BEING POOR IN THE CITY

In 1987 Brian Branche left his family for three months to live in the inner city. He lived on £49 a week, the same as the dole, and he only took with him a sleeping bag, a change of clothes, a prayer book and a Bible.

I went to the inner city as a journalist. But I wasn't asking 'How do you feel?' I wanted to become poor. It was a sort of incarnation. When I knew what poverty did to me then I would have some idea what it did to other

The Revd Brian Branche

Brian Branche is married to Jose and they have two married children, three foster children and one grandchild. Brian has had a rich and varied career: boy-entrant, RAF; amateur boxer; engineer; factory worker; chimney sweep; film extra; merchant navy; Post Office engineer; and now a priest of the Church of England. His interests are sculpture, art, sports, camping and living!

people, and the insights which that gave to me I could give to the church. If the church is the sign of the kingdom then it has to be biassed and it has to be good news to the poor.

I wanted to find out what poverty means and what the desert in the city means. I also wanted to find out what faith in the city means and what relying on God means, and what hope means to someone in a hopeless situation, with not much money and no family and no friends.

So I left behind the people and the things which affirm me. My dog-collar was one of them. It is a sign and a symbol which people recognize. They might be critical of it or positive towards it, but it gives me an identity as a person in a structured organization.

I am a family man, and the people in this community know me as a husband and a father and a friend. All those things help to reassure me as the person who I am. So I wanted to leave all those identities behind. I wore a fisherman's smock, jeans and sandals.

When people don't know your background and you haven't got a story to tell you don't have an identity, so people don't trust you. You are a strange man who they are suspicious of— and then you feel vulnerable. You realize that people are looking at you. 'Is he a tramp?' they are wondering, 'Is he a con man. . . is he unemployed. . . is he a useless hangalong to society?'

First of all I went to Tottenham and stayed at the YMCA in Hornsey. It was geared up for the unemployed. Over fifty per cent of us were black. There were quite a few ex-offenders and ex-drug-users and also the normal run of the mill people who use the YMCA.

Nobody in the hostel knew who I was so I was treated like everybody else. Quite often I would be pushed around, in other places as well as the hostel. They just thought I was unemployed, and because of that if I went to ask a question they would say, 'Move away! We're too busy. We'll deal with you later on.'

I had to learn to queue up for my food and for other things. When my money was getting low I would wait around and if something came over the loudspeaker to say there was some casual labour going I had to run down with the others — and it was a case of first come first served. So we would all push and shove to get down the steps.

What did you feel like when you lost your identity and were there with all those people?

Depressed and scared. I felt powerless. I didn't have an agenda — and the agenda I had on my desk when I started out just wasn't there any more.

The desert looks romantic when you aren't in it. But when you are in the heat of the sun it is different. The parched land is crying out for water, and you are desperately thirsty, and all of a sudden it shows you how vulnerable you are. That's scarey. It is something to do with death-making.

Sometimes when people looked at me I just wanted to shout out. Because I looked unemployed by my dress people who were better dressed got served first, even when I was next in the queue. I was sometimes told to wait, and I would want to shout out and say, 'I'm a vicar. . .I'm not a tramp.'

* * *

So if there is any encouragement in Christ, any incentive of love, any participation in the Spirit, any affection and sympathy, complete my joy by being of the same mind, having the same love. . . Do nothing from selfishness or conceit, but in humility count others better than yourselves. Let each of you look not only to his own interests, but also to the interests of others.

Have this mind among yourselves, which is yours in Christ Jesus, who, though he was in the form of God, did not count equality with God a thing to be grasped, but emptied himself, taking the form of a servant, being born in the likeness of men. (Philippians 2:1–7)

IMAGINE* . . . that you are a homeless person in an inner city. You have no family or friends, and you are very poor. Your clothes are scruffy and a bit smelly. How do people look at you when they see you? What does the look on their face make you feel? How would Jesus look at you? What would the look on his face make you feel?

Bishop Ronald Bowlby — 1/Saturday

THE HOMELESS

'A man was going down from Jerusalem to Jericho, and he fell among robbers, who stripped him and beat him, and departed, leaving him half dead.

'Now by chance a priest was going down that road; and when he saw him he passed by on the other side. So likewise a Levite, when he came to the place and saw him, passed by on the other side.

'But a Samaritan, as he journeyed, came to where he was; and when he saw him, he had compassion, and went to him and bound up his wounds, pouring on oil and wine; then he set him on his own beast, and brought him to an inn, and took care of him. And the next day he took out two denarii and gave them to the innkeeper, saying, "Take care of him; and whatever more you spend, I will repay you when I come back." ' (Luke 10:30–35)

If I have any real sense of our fundamental equality before God, how can I walk by on the other side if my brother or my sister is in the ditch and without

Bishop Ronald Bowlby

Ronald Bowlby is married to Elizabeth and they have three sons and two daughters. He is deeply concerned about homelessness and speaks on this and other issues in the House of Lords. He is an active campaigner for the ordination of women to the priesthood and likes hill-walking and listening to music. He is the Anglican Bishop of Southwark.

shelter? Being mugged and left at the side of the road is about being injured and interrupted on a journey — but it is also about being without shelter, and the wounded man was taken to the inn and given shelter so that he could recover.

It does seem to me that to have shelter and to have warmth in a place where you can rear and nurture a family and look after the elderly is really one of the most fundamental human requirements, next to having enough food to live on and clothes for your back.

I would like Christians first of all to look at their own area. We are all being exhorted to do parish audits, and I think people are a bit alarmed and not quite sure what it's all about — and they are wondering whether it is actually going to help the gospel. But I think on this issue a group of Christians from local churches could very profitably (with some help, which wouldn't be difficult to get) actually look at their own town or country district or inner city area and see what is happening about the housing needs of old people, young people and various other people in the community.

Just one of the things they will discover is that single people have no statutory right to be housed or sheltered at all. I think there is often an assumption in people's minds that all single people who are homeless must be feckless, so why should we worry about them? 'They are all meths drinkers sitting on the seat in the park.' Now in fact they represent 5 to 10 per cent of the problem. They are often very sad, unhappy people who have been discharged from mental hospitals to have 'community care', which is then not in fact available.

A lot of single homeless people are youngsters who have left home — and not because they have been so awful that they have been kicked out. Perhaps their parents' marriage has broken down and someone else has moved in, and all kinds of things have happened which have made it impossible for that youngster to stay at home.

The single homeless may simply be people who moved to try and get a job, and managed for a bit but then were asked to leave the digs they were in and couldn't get anything else so they lost their job. The stories are legion. That is just one little bit of this whole problem.

Christians can try to find out what happens to a young married couple who can't afford to buy a home, and what is happening to these single people who are perhaps unemployed. They can just start off by getting the facts and figures from the local authorities and from the housing associations and from talking to people. Then I think very often they will realize that homelessness and bad housing are far more serious and widespread than they had any idea about. That is often just as true in the country as it is in the towns and the inner cities.

Then perhaps this group of Christians could look at some of the ways in which the problem is being tackled. They could learn a bit about local authority housing and housing associations and the 'private sector' houses to rent, and then discover how little or how much contribution these various bodies make, how much different kinds of housing cost, and why things are as they are.

It would be very good for Christians in a locality actually to address how things are where *they* are. In the process they might well learn enough about this to feel, 'Well, we really have to do something: and we need to bring pressure on our MP or local councillor; or perhaps we can work with a housing association, or even conceivably try to set one up.'

In one way or another I wonder if people can just find face-to-face ways of discovering what we are talking about when we are talking about homelessness.

IMAGINE* just for a few moments that you have nowhere to live and hardly any money. Shut your eyes and see what you feel like. What would you do? What would you like other people to do?

'Truly I say to you, as you did it to one of the least of these my brethren, you did it to me.' (Matthew 25:40)

I'M A PERSON TOO

A FRIEND OF MINE had rheumatoid arthritis, and when it was at its worst her husband would push her round in a wheel-chair. People would then smile kindly at her, but address their questions to her husband. 'How is she. . .?', they would ask him, or 'Does she like sugar in her tea. . .?' Since the disease had affected her hips and not her head she found this treatment enormously irritating.

Society does this sort of un-personing all the time. Not just to a person who is in a wheel-chair but to any person who is different. A disabled person and an old person will often suffer from the indignity and so will a poor person. Then there is the person who for one reason or another some sections of society look down on or disapprove of.

Society hasn't changed very much, and two thousand years ago the religious people criticized Jesus for the way he treated the people at the bottom of the heap: 'Behold, a glutton and a drunkard, a friend of tax collectors and sinners. . .' (Luke 7:34).

But every person in the whole world is still a human being made in the image of God, however damaged they are by sickness or by sin, and whether it is their fault or someone else's. If we will dare to look into their eyes we shall hear the cry of their heart: 'I'm a person too. . .'

HOW CAN I ABANDON YOU?

The Jewish prophet Hosea shows us what God is like out of his own experience of being a parent. . . a father whose son is behaving very badly. . . and the father's having a real struggle to decide how to treat him.

The Lord says, 'When Israel was a child, I loved him and called him out of Egypt as my son. But the more I called to him, the more he turned away from me. My people sacrificed to Baal; they burnt incense to idols. Yet I was the one who taught Israel to walk. I took my people up in my arms, but they did not acknowledge that I took care of them. I drew them to me with affection and love. I picked them up and held them to my cheek; I bent down to them and fed them. . . How can I give you up, Israel? How can I abandon you?. . . My heart will not let me do it! My love for you is too strong. I will not punish you in my anger; I will not destroy Israel again. For I am God and not man. . .' (Hosea 11:1–4, 8–9 GNB)

Hosea is looking back into the past. . .remembering what it was like at the beginning. . .how much he loved his baby son. . .and what it was like to help him to take his first wobbling footsteps. . .with Hosea holding one of his hands. . .and then just a few triumphant steps and a crow of delight before he sat down on his bottom again. . .

In that memory, treasured away in Hosea's mind, he sees into the heart of God. . .God's enormous love for his son Israel. . . The heartache that it is to remember what it was like at the beginning. . . when everything seemed to be going right.

It was the same heartache of remembering that Hosea has for his wife. . .when she'd gone off with her lovers. And first of all he gets furious with her. . .but then he starts working out how to get her back again. . .

I'm going to take her back into the desert again; there I will win her back with words of love. I'll give back to her the vineyards she had, and make Trouble Valley a door of hope. She will respond to me there as she did when she was young. . . Then once again she'll call me her husband. . .
(2:14–16)

Hosea had one of the deepest prophetic insights into the heart of God that there's ever been. . . God isn't a philosophical abstraction. . .God's a lover, who goes on loving his wife when she's unfaithful and his son when he leaves home and abandons him.

Jesus also told us about a father whose son had left home. . .in maybe the best loved of all his stories: the prodigal son, who went away from his father into a far country. A German pastor called Helmut Thielike wrote a book about that and called it *The Waiting Father* — with God the Father at the centre of the story.

We only sometimes see things from God's point of view. We mostly see them from ours: *us* as the prodigal son. . .and the relief for us when *we* get home. But Hosea and Jesus let us into the secret of the heart of God. . . the heart of Father. . . that's aching for us to come home again. . .whatever we've done. . .and he never stops loving us, and he can't bear to give us up.

PRAYER Father, help me to realize how much you mind. . .how much you yearn over me. . .and how much you love me. Let me not break your heart. . . Let me delight it instead. . .

Ruth Sims 2/Monday

AIDS SUFFERERS

When I came to the final interview for this post at the Mildmay I had not intended to tell them about my personal life. But they asked me about it and said they wanted to give the time to hearing about it. When I had finished telling them all about what had happened their comment was, 'What a tremendous amount you have to offer to people with broken lives'. I could not believe it. When I got the post, that was acceptance, and acceptance in a fundamentally evangelical Christian hospital. I felt that if they could see fit to appoint me as their nursing director then I could start forgiving myself.

Before I came to the Mildmay in April 1987 I had never really addressed the issues of homosexuality. I had a couple of friends whom I knew were gay. I loved them. If I'm honest it wasn't something that I liked to think about too much in the context of them as people. But it made no difference.

Exactly one year later, as I have listened to people who are in this situation, and really talked with them, all I can say is, 'There but for the grace of God go I' — given their life, their home, their circumstances, the things that have influenced their lives, their environment, and the way they are. Everyone wouldn't necessarily agree with me, but I don't believe that people would honestly *choose* a homosexual lifestyle. There are far too many losses inherent in being homosexual to make that the first choice for anybody.

I was asked by a gay man how I would feel if my son were to come to me and tell me he was a homosexual. I would feel incredibly sad. I wouldn't feel horror or distaste or any of those things. What I think I would feel for him would be a terrible sadness at the losses that his life would have.

I believe that with God everything is possible, but at the same time I am concerned about the Christians I have seen struggling to be heterosexual, and having girl friends and trying to live a 'normal' lifestyle. But it hasn't been 'normal' for them. So in opting for celibacy, because they believe the Bible teaches that this is the right option for the Christian, they are committing themselves to a life without any physical expression of feelings of love that they may have. This must be a terribly hard road to tread, and a road that many Christians feel they have to walk alone without the understanding and support of family and friends.

Many people who have come to me from within the church have wept, because they have shared with me that they have these tendencies themselves. They have been coping alone with this for their whole life. Now why do they talk to me? I believe it is because they know that I have addressed these issues. They know that I will accept them as they are and that I am prepared to listen. The fact that they have been unable to share within their church family is so sad.

I spent a month in San Francisco with the hospice programme, and I discovered that most of the 50,000 gay men who are HIV+ are not San Franciscans. They have gone there to find acceptance, and a unity with people who will accept them. In 1988/89 we shall have over 750 people dying of AIDS in London. But they won't all be Londoners. Many are homosexuals and drug-users who have come here because they have known rejection from

Mrs Ruth Sims

Ruth Sims is Director of Nursing at the Mildmay Mission Hospital in London's East End which houses Europe's first hospice for people with AIDS. She worked with the San Francisco AIDS hospice programme and also spent time in Edinburgh looking at the needs of drug-users who have AIDS. She has four children and likes music, walking and the theatre.

their family and from their community, and in some instances from the church in particular.

The first thing that we as Christians have got to do is to go out to these people and offer them friendship and unconditional love. Jesus would have shown them love and compassion. And they need so much love. They have known rejection and isolation. I have known rejection for eighteen months, but many of them have known rejection and isolation for most of their lives. Many have been seeking, I believe, in their promiscuity to find somebody for whom they can be the most important person in the world. Isn't this something we all need and hope for?

There don't seem to be many people in churches to whom youngsters can go to if they have homosexual tendencies and I think that's because we see this as a shock-horror situation. We don't present as loving, caring people who can take *anything* on board.

What I think we could do as individuals and as churches is to discuss the issues concerned with AIDS and the people that we are going to care for who have it. Showing that we are concerned enough to be dealing with these issues openly, even if only at a discussion level, will mean that people will see us as more approachable: we have taken the problem on board and we are trying to identify what we can do about it.

We need to link up with other groups who are dealing with people with AIDS. I think we need to link up with them and say 'What can we do?' Let us work together. The people living with AIDS at Mildmay need love and a safe environment. Many of them have spiritual pain and spiritual problems. We don't spend time condemning and judging people. We give love and care to them, praying to God to help us, trusting his Holy Spirit to work in our lives and in the lives of those we touch.

* * *

A PRAYER **Searching**

Do you know what it is like
To search for someone to love
and never find someone?

Why, O God,	Where have you been?
Did it take this	Where have I been?
To make me	Is it too late for me?
Find myself?	Is there still a chance?

(Carl Burke)

'Then (the King) will say to those on his left, "Away from me, you that are under God's curse! Away to the eternal fire which has been prepared for the Devil and his angels! I was hungry but you would not feed me, thirsty but you would not give me a drink; I was a stranger but you would not welcome me in your homes, naked but you would not clothe me; I was sick and in prison but you would not take care of me."

'Then they will answer him, "When, Lord, did we ever see you hungry or thirsty or a stranger or naked or sick or in prison, and would not help you?" The King will reply, "I tell you, whenever you refused to help one of these least important ones, you refused to help me." These, then, will be sent off to eternal punishment, but the righteous will go to eternal life.'

(Matthew 25:41–46 GNB)

Ruth Sims 2/Tuesday

THEY CROSSED OVER THE ROAD

When it became quite impossible for my husband and I to live together we knew that the most important thing was to keep the children together as a unit. What I wanted to do was to remain at home and look after them. But one of us had to go, and it had to be me — and it looked to everyone as if I had just walked out of the family home and left my husband to it. My husband is a headmaster and incredibly good with children, and I knew that if I went my mother-in-law would be involved for twelve hours a day. She had been very good as a child-minder, and she would be there. But it looked as if I didn't care.

The Health Authority found me a flat fourteen miles away. To start off with there was no telephone, and I couldn't afford to go home very often. The idea was that if my husband and I separated and had some time apart to think things out then we would be able to get back together again. But I was totally isolated, and I did my grieving for the loss of my family and children in a situation where I was completely alone. I didn't know what to do.

After I had moved out I felt I couldn't go to our church because of what people would think of me, and I didn't feel I could talk to them about it. When I had been in my flat for three weeks I had the phone put in. But nobody rang me from the church. Nobody wrote and nobody came to see me. I had been to that church since I was 2½ years old. I had been the Girl's Brigade Captain, the youth club leader and the missionary secretary.

But nobody contacted me. They would ask my husband to lunch, or make him cakes and put them on the doorstep. So my feeling of isolation was reinforced. If just one person had come and said, 'Why aren't you coming to church?' I might have thought, 'Maybe I am being silly and maybe I should go. . .'

I began to feel that to communicate with God was useless. I felt incredibly guilty — although as a child who had grown up with incest (I was adopted) and child abuse to the age of fourteen I was used to living with guilt. Children who are abused learn to live with it. That might have had something to do with the break-up of our marriage. Yet if anybody had been prepared to help us they might have identified it and perhaps been able to help us to deal with it. I have never been unfaithful to my husband and I have never been interested in other men. I wouldn't have put any man I was friendly with in the position of being accused of bad behaviour. But this guilt that I lived with now my marriage had broken up meant that I really felt a hypocrite praying or ever expecting that anything good would happen.

When after a year I found my absence from the children intolerable I got the opportunity of a mortgage to buy a flat, so I moved back into the area. One day I was walking down the street and I saw a man and his wife that I knew from the church coming along towards me. But when they saw me they crossed over the road.

Then I thought I just can't go back to that church because nobody cares about me and nobody has wanted to help me. They have all been very prepared to make judgements about me based on assumptions, and nobody has even bothered to come and find out the truth about the situation. I found this increasingly hard. But I think the Holy Spirit was working, and I began to feel that I had to worship God. So I went to the nearest Baptist church. I spoke to the minister there and told him my story. He said, 'Well, Ruth, I suppose that as a Christian I should tell you that reconciliation with your husband would be the best thing; but within the church we are increasingly realizing that marriages sometimes break apart, and then we have to help people as individuals and not as a couple.'

He said he would speak to my own minister, and I actually went back to my former church the following Sunday with all my children. I spoke to some of the people there and I think God enabled me to be incredibly direct. I asked them why they hadn't contacted me or helped me. The answer they gave me was that they felt this was something right outside their experience. And the couple who had crossed over the road said it was worse than seeing someone who was bereaved, because they simply didn't know what to say. They told me they were incredibly sad about it all, but because it was outside their experience as a church and as individuals they didn't know what to do.

I could understand that. But I said that the church must somehow manage to take this on board. We need to face the fact that some Christians are going to have serious marriage problems and start finding out how we can help them. Maybe some people within the church should be learning how to help, or at least finding out where people with these problems can be helped. They need to know that we can listen to them, whatever their problem is. It can never be right to bury our heads in the sand, or turn away from a person because their problem is outside our experience. It only needed one or two people to say to me, 'We don't understand Ruth, but we care'. It would have made a world of difference. It might even have prevented what happened.

When I got the post at Mildmay the acceptance that I found within this group of Christians made an enormous difference. Realizing that God had forgiven me and was being creative with my life did a whole lot for me. But I was very worried and I kept talking about the effect this breakdown must inevitably have on the children.

Then Dr Veronica Moss, the Medical Director here, said something that really helped: 'You trust so many things to the Lord in your daily life, and he takes care of them. Have you not thought that you can trust your children to him? Leave them there with him and ask him to heal their hurts. He can do it, Ruth.' I did that, and I believed it.

Subsequently my relationship with my children has been restored in a way that I could never have believed possible. I have had an opportunity to talk with them all, even the smallest one, and tell them how incredibly sad their father and I were, and how unhappy I was not to be with them. I wanted to be with them as much as they wanted to be with me.

I had taken it for granted that the children knew how hurt I was, but they didn't. It wasn't until I cried with them that they realized how much I hurt. I had thought that if they didn't want to come round to see me, or if they weren't around, then if I let them see how much it mattered I was restricting their freedom. So I would say, 'That's all right. You go and see your friends.' Then I realized that I also had to say, 'Well, I really had hoped so much to see you. . .' Otherwise it looked as if I didn't care. Then things started to be restored. They had obviously thought it didn't matter to me, and they have had to learn as children that adults can hurt a lot.

We all make mistakes in our lives, but God can be creative even with the mistakes. What I have tried to tell the children is that 'Daddy and I did make mistakes and we didn't treat each other properly': to make them realize that we're not perfect and that because we're not then things can go wrong. But we have to do the best we can with the things that are not perfect, and with God's help we can be creative with the mistakes that we have made. Because that is what God is. So if you know of someone who is going or has gone through a break-up of their marriage, please don't judge them. Please talk with them and pray for them.

'Fear not, O land;
be glad and rejoice,
for the Lord has done great things!
Fear not, you beasts of the field,
for the pastures of the wilderness are green;
the tree bears its fruit,
the fig tree and vine give their full yield.

'Be glad, O sons of Zion,
and rejoice in the Lord, your God;
for he has given the early rain for your vindication,
he has poured down for you abundant rain,
the early and the latter rain, as before.

'The threshing floors shall be full of grain,
the vats shall overflow with wine and oil.
I will restore to you the years
which the swarming locust has eaten. . .

'You shall eat in plenty and be satisfied,
and praise the name of the Lord your God,
who has dealt wonderously with you.'
(Joel 2:21–26)

A PRAYER* Lord Jesus Christ, you came to bind up the brokenhearted. I pray for the people I know whose marriages are broken, and perhaps whose hearts are broken as well. . . I pray for the children of those marriages. . . And I pray for anyone who has a broken marriage but who has no one to pray for her, or for him. . . I hold that person whom I have never met in your healing presence. . .

Christopher Nolan — 2/Wednesday

A DISABLED PERSON?

Christopher Nolan is 21. He nearly died at birth from asphyxiation. But he survived, with severe brain damage. He cannot speak; he cannot hear well; and he cannot move himself. After an enormous struggle he learned to type, with a stick attached to his head, and this year his book *Under the Eye of the Clock* (Weidenfeld & Nicolson, £8.95) won the prize for the Whitbread Book of the Year.

Under the Eye of the Clock **is really the incredible story of Christopher**

Mr Christopher Nolan

Christopher Nolan was born and lives in Ireland. He was educated in Dublin at the Central Remedial Clinic School, Mount Temple Comprehensive and at Trinity College. *Dam-Burst of Dreams*, collected poems and other writings, was published in 1981. His writing has been compared to Joyce, Yeats and Dylan Thomas, and Professor John Carey, in his preface to this autobiography, describes Nolan as 'a brilliantly gifted young writer'. (Another photograph: p.31.)

Nolan's childhood, although he disguises himself and tells his story as if it were fiction.

'Can you credit all of the fuss that was made of a cripple, mused Joseph Meehan as he settled his back against the seat for the flight home to Dublin.' He is on his way back from London, where he has won an award from the British Spastics Society for his book of poems and other writings, *Dam-Burst of Dreams*. His writing has been compared to Joyce, Yeats and Dylan Thomas. But the struggle and the pain to get there was beyond believing. When he goes to school he dreads the reaction of the other children.

'He imagined what the pupils would be thinking when his voice would involuntarily ring out a screech associated with tension or what, he worried, will they think when my arms fly outstretched when they try pushing my wheelchair through the crowded corridors or, worst of all, will they think I'm bonkers if my hands suddenly fly forward and hit them in the face. . .?'

Often the pain of everything is so awful that he cries bitter tears. His mother puts him in his chair and then sits down to talk to him.

'Looking through his tears he saw her as she bent low in order to look into his eyes. "I never prayed for you to be born crippled," she said, "I wanted you to be full of life, able to run and jump and talk just like Yvonne. But you are you, you are Joseph not Yvonne. Listen here Joseph, you can see, you can hear, you can think, you can understand everything you hear, you like your food, you like nice clothes, you are loved by me and Dad. We love you just as you are." Pussing still, snivelling still, he was listening to his mother's voice.

She spoke sort of matter-of-factly but he blubbered moaning sounds. His mother had her say and that was that. She got on with her work while he got on with his crying.

'The decision arrived at that day was burnt forever in his mind. He was only three years in age but he was now fanning the only spark he saw, his being alive and more immediate, his being wanted just as he was.'

Later on, before he goes to Dublin, he has a conversation with God.

'What am I going to do when I leave here, he voiced out loud. . . What will happen when I go to Dublin's Central Remedial Clinic School? What will become of me when I have nobody to understand my talkstyle? What will my teachers make of me? I'm afraid, are you listening, don't see and say nothing. I'm afraid, afraid of my life 'cause I won't have mam or dad or even Yvonne. I'll be on my own, my head falling back and forward, not able to talk, not able to hug myself when I get afraid. God, would you be afraid if you were me?'

One of his comforts is communion.

'Communion too brought his comforter within his grasp and in close body contact he created silent desperate credence. Communion served grand purpose, serving to bring God to him and him to servile God.

'Fr John Flynn was curate in Clontarf. Every Wednesday and Sunday he called to Joseph's house and in his inside pocket he carried the pyx bearing the consecrated bread. God assumed beautiful credit by breathing love through the eucharist. Candlelight burned as the priest began his polished prayers of terrible beauty. Then, holding aloft the white host, he expressed Joesph's prayer of pleading:

> Lord, I am not worthy to receive you,
> but only say the word and I shall be healed.'

When Christopher Nolan received his prize for that book his mother gave the acceptance speech which he had written, and he used it to speak about the handicapped and about abortion.

'Tonight a crippled man is taking his place on the world literary stage. Tonight is my night for laughing, for crying tears of joy. But wait, my brothers hobble after me hinting, "What about silent us? Can we too have a voice?" Tonight I am speaking for them.

'Tonight is the happiest night of my life. Imagine what I would have missed if the doctors had not revived me on that September day long ago.'

A PERSON CALLED ENID

Last Saturday Enid walked very slowly into the elegant fish restaurant. Her son supported her on one side and her daughter-in-law on the other. They sat her down on the red, plush chair and the waiter put the menu in front of her. Somehow the meal got chosen, and then I heard snatches of the conversation. . .

'They're nice people in the place where you live, aren't they?' (the question carefully phrased so as not to refer to the 'home'. . .)

'Yes', she said quietly.

'You do talk to them, don't you?'

'Yes, sometimes', she said.

'And you go down and sit with them sometimes, don't you?'

'Sometimes', she said — and I found myself thinking that any interviewer on the media who asked questions like that would get either the sack or a severe telling-off. Questions that can only be answered by 'Yes' or by 'No' are bad questions. The right questions draw information out of the person. But perhaps they didn't want to know that the other people in the home were not very nice and that Enid didn't like them very much.

Enid ate her fish rather slowly.

'Don't hurry', they exhorted her loudly. 'There's no need to hurry. . .' She went on eating — delicately, carefully.

'Aren't you going to finish your wine?', they asked — kindly, but a bit reproachfully, as if speaking to a small girl. She didn't say anything, but picked it up and sipped it.

'Yes, good. . .that's right. . .I would if I was you. . .', said the daughter-in-law approvingly, in the tone of voice that the Nannies of previous generations must have used to their charges.

The final conversation came after I had returned from the Ladies Cloakroom, right at the top of two narrow flights of stairs, and I had just finished telling my friends what a long way up it was. The question of whether or not Enid wished to go to the Ladies was being discussed at the next table, and one of my friends got involved.

'It's a long way up', she said, 'I don't think she'll manage it. . .'

By then the son, who had just been to the Gents, came back, and his wife shared the difficulty with him.

'She won't be able to get there', she told him. Then she addressed Enid. 'What we'll do', she said, 'is just to go for a *short* drive, and then we'll take you back.'

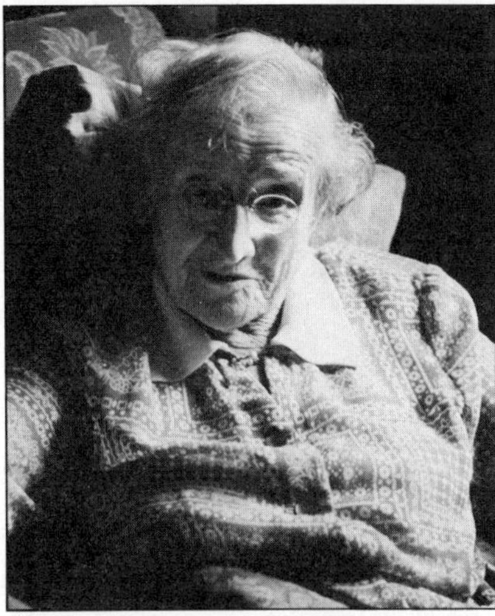

'A Person called Enid'

Mrs Hilda Vincent, the Chief Officer of Age Concern in Croydon, told me how much the churches could help if they would work with the professionals in Age Concern. She fears we have exchanged the workhouse for the old people's home. In Croydon there are over 50,000 elderly people. In Britain there are millions — each one a person made in the image and likeness of God.

N.B. This is not 'Enid', but simply a picture of an old, beautiful woman.

'Perhaps we could find somewhere else. . .' said the son, rather helplessly. 'I'll go and get the car and bring it round. . .'

I felt indignant on Enid's behalf. Why hadn't they checked where the loo was? How would either of them have liked to go on a drive (even if it was now going to be a disappointingly shorter one) longing to go to the loo? Why couldn't they ask her proper questions so that she could give them proper answers? Why, since she couldn't see very well, couldn't they pull the straggly white hairs out of Enid's chin?

Why couldn't they see the person that Enid still was?

As the clear light is upon the holy candlestick so is the face in ripe age.
(Ecclesiasticus 26:17)

A MEDITATION Imagine that you are Enid and sitting at that table with your son and daughter-in-law. What do you feel like? What do you feel about them? Did you really want to go there at all, or would you rather have done something else? If Jesus was sitting opposite to you at the table, how do you think he would have treated you?

'I'M A WIDOW...'

Alec died nearly twenty months ago. . . I am still counting in months. He died in my arms, very quickly and very peacefully. He died at home, which was what we had always hoped for. We had said, 'No more hospitals', because it was so important to be at home and to be together.

Part of the feeling that I had was rather strange. It was almost a sense of relief — that something we had anticipated and almost rehearsed had actually happened. We had lived with the thought of his death from the time we had married, because he had heart trouble. We thought we might have a year together, and we thought that would be good. But we had ten years, which was ten times more than we had ever dared to hope for. Over those years we had lived with the possibility of death, and now it had happened. But immediately after that strange reaction of relief there was desperate sadness — and disbelief and pain and anger. . .

Alec was the focal point of my life and I was the focal point of his, and it was the loss of that which was the saddest thing of all. It was at the heart of all my sadness. At first a lot of people came in to see me and supported me, and did all sorts of things, and allowed me to cry. I have got quite a large family and a lot of friends, and I was very loved and cared for. But when that begins to go you suddenly find yourself with this awful label. . . 'I'm a widow. . .' You are not exactly second class, but you are much less important. Like a lot of other older women you have joined the gang. There are an awful lot of us about, and you're just one more. So there is a kind of loss of status in society — and a widow of some months' standing is different from someone who is newly widowed, and different again from someone who is married. I am beginning now to meet people who have never known me married. They have only known me as a widow, and I don't like that.

I still chuckle about the things that I know Alec would laugh at, so in a way I can still share things with him. But I miss him; desperately sometimes; and I think that I shall always miss him. It's not the sort of miss that is on the surface, but you know that however good your life is, and however loving your friends and children may be, nevertheless somewhere inside you there is a bit of you that's empty. And that's just a reality that you have to learn to adjust to.

So long as I am feeling all right about myself I don't feel a bit second class. I have a lot of interests, and there are many strands to my life and I have my work. It is only when I am feeling very vulnerable and missing Alec desperately that I feel terribly second class and not worth very much.

But even when I am feeling all right about myself I still have to deal with the really painful bits. And I have to do that alone — not with anybody else. However good society is, and however caring and however marvellous, the actual pain of that separation and that empty place inside me are just mine. No one else can deal with that for me. When the pain is very bad what I try to do is just to be still and feel or react. . . If I want to sit and howl my eyes out then I will. Whatever I feel I want to do I just do it. I don't try to escape.

One of the things Alec used to say was, 'It will pass. . .' Bad times do pass, and that's quite useful to hang on to. It will pass. But I don't want to push it away. I like to stay with it. I don't want to miss out on even the hard and the painful bits. But sometimes it's pretty horrid. . .

* * *

At the Jewish Feast of Harvest, the festival at which in the New Testament the Holy Spirit was poured out on the Day of Pentecost, the instructions for the keeping of the feast say that everyone is to be included in the celebration.

'You shall count seven weeks; begin to count the seven weeks from the time you first put the sickle to the standing grain. Then you shall keep the feast of weeks to the Lord your God with the tribute of a freewill offering from your hand, which you shall give as the Lord your God blesses you; and you shall rejoice before the Lord your God, you and your son and your daughter, your manservant and your maidservant, the Levite who is within your towns, the sojourner, the fatherless, and the widow who are among you, at the place which the Lord your God will choose, to make his name dwell there. You shall remember that you were a slave in Egypt; and you shall be careful to observe these statutes.' (Deuteronomy 16:9–12)

REFLECT 'Religion that is pure and undefiled before God and the Father is this: to visit orphans and widows in their affliction, and to keep oneself unstained from the world' (James 1:27).

Paddy Yorkstone 2/Saturday

'WE DIE WITH THE DYING. . .'

Someone who is dying brings us up against our own fear: a fear that we all know; that one day we are going to die ourselves. Most of us don't want to think about that; so we retreat and look away. Not always, but often. And that can isolate the dying person terribly. Other people won't talk about it and they pretend it isn't happening.

I think the reason why a lot of people can't talk about death or about dying is that they don't feel safe to do so. Sometimes I will ask them, 'What can I do to help?' But it is important that whoever is helping has really looked at their own fears and hang-ups about dying. Because if we feel safe then we can talk about things and share things.

A young teenage friend of mine phoned up one day in a terrible state of anxiety. As part of her social studies at school she had heard a talk about death and dying, but the person teaching her group had obviously been very frightened of the whole thing. Consequently she had frightened everybody else, including this girl. But because I wasn't frightened of talking about it then when we spoke about it she could feel all right. That is what I mean about feeling safe.

It would be good if society could be more open about death. If we could start to take our children to funerals, for example. If you take your child to the funeral of somebody who isn't very important — a great aunt whom they have never met, perhaps — then a funeral and death becomes a normal and acceptable part of things. And we shouldn't hide our grief and our distress if somebody is very ill. When my own mother was dying of cancer and had an operation my children were only little, and they were very upset. I said to them that Gran was very ill; and the doctors couldn't make her better but they could make her comfortable. We talked about it, and we could be open. If I had hidden my fear and my distress it would have created more fear and distress in them, and it would have become a vicious circle.

Alec and I had lived with dying and the possibility of it, and what I want to say about dying is that it's all right to hurt — both as a widow and as

Mrs Paddy Yorkstone

Paddy Yorkstone was the bereavement service co-ordinator at St Christopher's Hospice. She now does some training of bereavement counsellors and people involved in hospice work, and has retrained in therapeutic massage. She has two sons and a daughter by her first marriage, and her second husband died nearly two years ago. She has five grandchildren and two cats.

somebody who is dying. It is very painful to be a widow. It is agonizing and terrible. And it is agonizing and terrible to know that you are going to lose your life. But hurting is all right. You are not going to fall apart at the seams. You can hurt and you can survive. It is important not to run away from hurt. It's awful; but it doesn't go on for ever. If you let it flow around you, and go wherever it takes you, then it's all right.

After Alec died a lot of people said to me, 'Now, you have been working with bereavement all these years. Has it made any difference to you? Has it helped you?' And I was able to say, 'Yes'. Because I had had a chance to be with the dying and the bereaved, and to sort out my own feelings, what that did for me was to give me the courage to do what I felt was right. When Alec died I wanted to keep his body at home and I said so. But earlier on if someone had said, 'I think you ought to get the undertakers to take him away', then I would have given in and said, 'Yes, I'm sure you are right'. But I wanted the children and the grandchildren to see his body. I just knew in my heart and my gut that it was right to keep him at home, so I went along with it. So whereas before I would have responded to outside pressures, my work at St Christopher's gave me the courage to do what I knew was right. That is what education and learning did for me; and that is what we need to do for other people.

* * *

A good name is better than precious ointment;
   and the day of death, than the day of birth.
It is better to go to the house of mourning
   than to go to the house of feasting;
for this is the end of all men,
   and the living will lay it to heart.
Sorrow is better than laughter,
   for by sadness of countenance the heart is made glad.
The heart of the wise is in the house of mourning;
   but the heart of fools is in the house of mirth.

(Ecclesiastes 7:1–4)

TO THINK ABOUT   We are afraid to live because we are afraid to die.

STUDY GROUP MATERIAL

I'm a person too

1. Begin with the Coventry Cathedral Prayer.

2. This section, 'I'm a person too', has looked at people who are disabled, divorced, widowed, old, dying, and who have AIDS. Are there any other people whom society un-persons? Why do we do it? Can it have anything to do with the fact that we are frightened of being like that ourselves? How did Jesus treat people? How could we treat them — and how would we like to be treated if we were in their shoes?

3. The piece about Christopher Nolan only has a very short scripture reading for the day.

> 'Lord I am not worthy to receive you,
> but only say the word and I shall be healed'
> (based on Matthew 8:8)

Healing is about wholeness. Who is the more whole: Christopher Nolan, or a person who fears a disabled person, a poor person, or a person dying from AIDS, and doesn't want to have anything to do with him or with her?

PRAYING

1. Use the imaginative meditation at the end of Thursday, 'A person called Enid'. Share what you felt, and how you would like to be treated.

2. Read out the passage at the end of Monday about the final judgement from Matthew 25. Sit in silence for a few minutes. Then share what came into your mind.

Week 3

SECOND CLASS CITIZENS

IT'S A WHITE MAN'S WORLD, so long as the white man isn't poor. The rest are second class citizens. As I drove to work this morning I heard on my car radio that women doctors don't get nearly so many of the top jobs as the men, because of the old boy network. In my own profession that is even more true, because at the moment women in the church don't even have a single top job — nor much likelihood of getting one in the foreseeable future.

But this section of *My World* isn't about women, although a lot of what is said can be applied to them. Once we know how we define a second class citizen, and how we treat them, then we can start to change our attitudes and our behaviour in every area. Even those of us who are part of the great majority, and *are* second class citizens, can still be fulfilled, loving human beings, not fretting our lives away thinking 'If only. . .'

But that side of the spiritual life isn't what this section is about either. It is about the way some of us treat second class citizens at the moment, and about how we ought to treat them. At the last judgement Christ will say one of two things to us: either, 'Truly, I say to you, as you did it to one of the least of these my brethren, you did it to me,' or else, 'Truly, I say to you, as you did it not to one of the least of these, you did it not to me' (Matthew 25:40, 45).

LIGHT OF ALL THE WORLD

He said to me, 'You are my servant, Israel through whom I shall win glory'; so I rose to honour in the Lord's sight, and my God became my strength. Once I said, 'I have laboured in vain; I have spent my strength for nothing, to no purpose'; yet in truth my cause is with the Lord and my reward is in God's hands. And now the Lord who formed me in the womb to be his servant, to bring Jacob back to him, that Israel should be gathered to him, now the Lord calls me again: it is too slight a task for you, as my servant, to restore the tribes of Jacob, to bring back the descendants of Israel: I will make you a light to the nations, to be my salvation to earth's farthest bounds. . .

(Isaiah 49:3–6 NEB)

The strange, suffering servant of God that Isaiah writes about and prophesies about is someone whom God forms in the womb of his mother. A servant who does the will of God and who the glory of God shines out of — and the glory's shining so that everyone can walk in the light of it. . .

In John 8:12 Jesus said, 'I am the light of the world,' and at the start of that gospel John writes of him as 'the real light that gives light to everyone. . .' (1:9). But we get possessive. It's *our* light, that *we've* seen, and it's shining inside *our* circle — not out there in the darkness. Us and them — shutting us in and them out — because we're the possessors and they aren't.

When I was at school they were always trying to get us to sit up straight, and if anyone managed to sit up for a whole term they were awarded a position girdle — a gold and navy blue ribbon to wear round their waist. Only one girl in our form had one — Jean. The rest of us slouched. So the teacher used to exhort us to do better, and as a way of persuading us one day she said, 'I'm quite sure Jean doesn't like being the only person in the class who's got a position girdle. . .' But Jean sat up even straighter and looked pleased with herself. . . 'Oh yes I do. . .I *like* being the only one. . .!'

And there's a bit in all of us, that likes hanging on to what we've got and being unique and exclusive. Like a child with a secret. It's her possession, and she only shares it with her best friend — and they draw a circle round them and keep everyone else out.

It isn't only children who do that. So do grown-ups. But if the secret they know is about the shining and the glory of God, they won't manage to keep everyone out — because the light wants to shine into everyone's darkness. The light of the knowledge of the glory of God and the love of God.

> He drew a circle to keep me out,
> Heretic, rebel a thing to flout.

But love and I had the wit to win:
We drew a circle that took him in.

Love sat down to eat with quislings and prostitutes and all the people that society didn't approve of, so that they weren't outside in the darkness any more — like the little matchgirl who looked in at the party from outside and desperately wanted to go in to it. Love let her in, and then told us, 'When you have a party, invite the poor, the crippled, the lame, the blind. . . then you will be blessed. . . God so loved the *world* that he gave his only Son. . .'

'I will make you a light to the nations, to be my salvation to earth's farthest bounds. . .' Perhaps that's where Jesus got those incredible words from — 'I am the light of the world. . . he who follows me shall not walk in darkness, but shall have the light of life. . .'

A PRAYER Suffering servant of God, shine into our darkness and give us the light of life. Then help us to shine as lights in the world. . . to love other people as you love us. . . and let the love of God be known throughout the whole earth. . .

Lord Scarman 3/Monday

SKIN DEEP

On the whole we are not an unjust society, but we do make mistakes. Sometimes those mistakes are deliberate, because of racial prejudice, and sometimes they are unconscious, because we don't realize what we are doing.

I do not believe that skin troubles are anything other than skin deep, and skin deep situations give way when they are faced with the strong relationships that can be built between individuals. If you put a black boy and a white boy together they will get on — assuming that they are both good, honest people.

I don't believe that you get bad relationships between black and white people except between groups. At the moment unemployment has a lot to do with the bad relationships between black and white. Even today there is still racial discrimination in job opportunities to the unemployed. There is a shortage of jobs, and when there is a vacancy to be filled there is discrimination in favour of white people over black people.

So I attach great importance to the education of employers. They must be made aware of the need to employ qualified black people if they present themselves. One of the practical ways to do this is to make sure that, when there is an agreed development project offering a large number of jobs, a good proportion of those jobs will go to black people. If that policy is followed then a large number of black employees will be taken on.

When the jobs are advertised it must be emphasized that the project is going to employ local labour. The employers shouldn't look outside for their labour force. They should look within the area of the inner city, where the development is happening — whether it is business, industry or whatever. I believe this is the way forward, rather than to pass legislation full of high-sounding principles which are immediately followed by provisos and exceptions.

There is still a tremendous amount of work to be done by the media and the leaders of our society. We need greater educational facilities, because when we have insufficient educational provision (just as when we have an insufficient health service) there will be some people who ought to be taken in but who are left out in the cold.

They will fall into the temptation of saying they have been discriminated against because of their colour. 'There are too many people helping the blacks; what about us poor whites. . .?' This white backlash is well known, and it arises out of deprivation.

Another aspect of race relations is the relationship between the police and the community. When I wrote the Brixton Report it wasn't difficult to discover the cause of the trouble. The police had come to the view that all public disorder and street mugging was arising in the black community, and in particular amongst the young black community. The young blacks saw the police as their enemies and the representatives of the establishment and determined to harass them on the streets.

But that picture has changed. The police are very well educated now in race relations. They really do understand their job professionally. And in some ways the young blacks are beginning to understand that their enemies are not the police. Their real enemies are much deeper seated problems in society.

So long as you have young, frustrated, largely male people who are driven to violence by their condition, so long will you have the police having to quell them and to arrest them, and the relationship between those two groups will suffer. But the solution is not to say, 'The police must mend their ways,' nor is it to say, 'The young black community must mend their ways.' The solution is an improvement of the whole environment, spiritual, moral, educational and of course physical.

The social problems that arise between the police and the black community are only one aspect of a general social problem, which I believe can only be tackled by improving the whole environment of the inner city.

* * *

Do not let class distinction enter into your faith in Jesus Christ, our glorified Lord. Now suppose a man comes into your synagogue, well-dressed and with a gold ring on, and at the same time a poor man comes in, in shabby clothes, and you take notice of the well-dressed man, and say, 'Come this way to the best seats'; then you tell the poor man, 'Stand over there' or 'You can sit on the floor by my foot-rest.' In making this distinction among yourselves have you not used a corrupt standard?

. . . It was those who were poor according to the world that God chose, to be rich in faith and to be the heirs to the kingdom which he promised to those who love him. You, on the other hand, have dishonoured the poor. Is it not the rich who lord it over you? Are not they the ones who drag you into court, who insult the honourable name which has been pronounced over you? Well, the right thing to do is to keep the supreme Law of scripture: you will love your neighbour as yourself; but as soon as you make class distinctions, you are committing sin and under condemnation for breaking the Law.

(James 2:1–9 NJB)

A PRAYER Imagine the desolation of an inner city area and the hopelessness of the people who live there. Then pray.

Almighty God, our heavenly Father,
we have sinned against thee,
through our own fault,
in thought, and word, and deed,
and in what we have left undone.
We are heartily sorry,
and repent of all our sins.
For thy Son our Lord Jesus Christ's sake,
forgive us all that is past,
and grant that we may serve thee in newness of life,
to the glory of thy name. Amen.

(ASB 1980)

Bishop Wilfred Wood 3/Tuesday

COLOURLESS AND COLOURED

Often when I have spoken on race and colour to audiences in this country, I have begun by saying: 'Now you have a choice of terms. We can either speak about "black" people and "white" people or we can speak about "coloured"

Bishop Wilfred Wood

Wilfred Wood and his wife Ina have 2 daughters and 3 sons. He is deeply concerned for children and people who are badly housed and is very active on their behalf. He is Chairman of the Martin Luther King Memorial Trust, and was Chairman of the Institute of Race Relations. He co-authored *Vicious Circle* with John Downing. He likes sport and is a keen supporter of Queen's Park Rangers. He says that he enjoys the sheer richness of human variety!

people and "colourless" people. Which one do you want to use?' Invariably the audience choose black and white. I think this is because although a person might not mind being considered 'white', he or she would not want to be 'colourless'!

I do this to point out that both groups of people see themselves as normal. Black and white are both colours, and that's that. But when you describe one group as 'white' and the other group as 'coloured' (which is not a colour) you are suggesting that anything other than white is a deviation from normal. Incidentally, I always insist on repeating the word 'people'. So we have unemployed *people*, not 'the Unemployed'; elderly *people* not 'the Elderly'; homeless *people*, not 'the Homeless'; black *people*, white *people*, disabled *people* and so on. We need all the help we can get to remind ourselves and others that in spite of differences, we are all *persons*. That is a profound theological statement.

It is easier for some of us to see this than for some other people. If like me you have grown up in the Caribbean where there is a mixture of various ethnic groups, a person's colour tells you as little about his intelligence, ability or humour as do his clothes! White people were a privileged minority, but none of us black people thought that wealth and privilege made white people superior! In fact, if you examine folk stories of the Caribbean you will see that they always depict the black man as being far cleverer than the white man. He is the little man whose cleverness is more than a match for the privileges of the powerful — a bit like Agatha Christie's detective stories where the policeman has the law and the resources, but it is Miss Marple or Poirot who manages to solve the crime!

There was this peculiar situation where all white cricket clubs and black cricket clubs and mixed cricket clubs all played each other in the same competitions, with no sense of threat and no particular desire to change anything. It is interesting that there was no hatred or acrimony on the part of black people against white. Even now, if you try to recall derogatory terms black people use for white people you will hardly find any, whereas there are numerous derogatory terms used by white people for black!

But there are many people who haven't had the experience of living in a multi-ethnic society. Until recently if you grew up in England you wouldn't have had any real or first-hand experience of black people. What you felt about them would largely depend on your cultural norms and what your history and geography books (written by white people) said about them. So you would be ignorant without knowing that you were ignorant, because for a number of vested-interest reasons, black people were normally projected as sub-human. Europeans who exploited Africa and inflicted degrading conditions of slavery and slaughter upon fellow human beings could only retain an image of themselves as civilized by pretending that black people were not human!

I wish I could say that all this was now behind us, but I remember a television programme which showed a young American soldier who had been serving in Vietnam paying a visit to his old school and being welcomed by flag-waving adoring children. He told them that he was out there fighting for freedom. He said: 'Vietnam is a lovely country. The one thing that is wrong with it is the people. They are not like us. They don't feel pain as we do. . .'

I think it is important that white people who presently have power, privilege and advantage in a terribly lopsided distribution of the necessities of life, should not think that it is only to the benefit of black people that there should be a better world. That kind of thinking leads at best to an attitude of *laissez-faire*, and at worst to opposition to peaceful efforts for change. A better world is a world better for all of us. In meeting our gaze no fellow human being should have to choose between a look of contempt and a look of fear. Invariably he will choose the latter and we will never break out of our present tail-spin of further draconian laws, more policemen, larger prisons, and ever-increasing crime.

* * *

For the foolishness of God is wiser than men, and the weakness of God is stronger than men. For consider your call, brethren; not many of you were wise according to worldly standards, not many were powerful, not many were of noble birth; but God chose what is foolish in the world to shame the wise, God chose what is weak in the world to shame the strong, God chose what is low and despised in the world, even things that are not, to bring to nothing things that are, so that no human being might boast in the presence of God. (1 Corinthians 1:25–29)

A PRAYER Look with love and mercy Lord, on my detractors and on me. If there is anything in me which rightly attracts their condemnation, please remove it. If without cause they fail in charity, forgive and restore them. For Christ's sake. Amen.

David Udo 3/Wednesday

THE DOWNTRODDEN HAVE A LOT TO GIVE

One of the fundamental beliefs of the Christian faith, expressed in the Bible, is that all men and women are created in the image of God and therefore of equal worth and value to him. Each person of whatever background or status has a role to play and a contribution to make to enrich the life of the society. Unfortunately, however, through misinterpretation even of the Bible and the distortion of our history, society has perpetuated a vicious circle of inequality and injustice and so placed certain sections of the society at a gross disadvantage.

There are people who quote the Bible to support their condescending attitude and contempt towards black people. The supporters of apartheid in South Africa for instance justify it biblically by saying that black people are the descendants of Ham, and the Bible says that the children of Ham were condemned to be hewers of wood and carriers of water. That rather narrow interpretation of the Bible is dangerous quite apart from being wrong. It has conditioned the minds of a lot of white 'Christians' in South Africa into accepting the notion of black inferiority.

Slavery and the slave trade have also made some people in this country believe in the notion of black inferiority. Through our history we know that all kinds of theories were produced in an effort to justify slavery. For instance, David Hume, a leading philosopher of the eighteenth century, claimed that black people were inferior, and he attempted to prove it. His philosophy and his theories came at the time when people like William Wilberforce and others were pressing for the abolition of slavery. But the slave trade was a very 'sound' economic venture, and it benefited England and the rest of Europe to keep it going. So if an outstanding and respected philosopher like David Hume came up with a theory of black inferiority then it would ease the Christian conscience.

This sort of thinking has continued in different forms to this day, leading to the conditioning of people's minds and attitudes. Therefore when there is an appeal for action to relieve poverty or a call for positive action against racial injustice, it is seen as doing black people a favour. But correcting any form of injustice in our society is not doing any one section a favour because injustice concerns *all* sections of the society. And we should not maintain the attitude of doing things *for* 'the less fortunate', for we are all less fortunate living in our present grossly unjust society.

There is a saying by a South American priest: 'When I give the poor food they call me a saint; but when I ask why the poor have no food they call me a Communist.' We should not be content with simply doing things for people any more than just taking palliatives and drugs to kill the pain and remove the symptom of an evil, cancerous disease in us. To get rid of the disease we have to get to the root of it. And when we look into the root causes of poverty, injustice and oppression we may find we have a part to play in them. Our attitude will therefore change from one of paternalism to that of genuine concern for the sake of the victim and for our sake as well; and our action will no longer be seen as a favour but as a necessity.

When people ask me, 'What should we do to help those in need?', I often think of the African proverb: 'If you give people a fish they will eat for a day; if you teach them to fish they will eat for a year.' Some people who quote this proverb usually stop there. But it goes on: 'And if you enable the people to develop the technique of fishing for themselves they will eat for the rest of their lives.'

Mr David Udo

David Udo is the Director of the Southwark Diocese Race Relations Commission. He is married with three daughters. He has studied theology and was Director of the Martin Luther King Memorial Trust (UK). He has been a school teacher, a community worker, and an employment and personnel consultant. He was associate editor of *Africa Challenge*, an African Christian publication. A Methodist local preacher, he enjoys reading, popular music and travelling.

We have to get people directly involved in seeking a solution to their situation. Part of the reason why the race relations industry in this country has failed to tackle racism in any effective way is that it has tended to *define* and *decide* and *do things for* the people who are the victims of racism. It has failed to realize that the people themselves should be involved in the process of seeking the solution towards changing the situation and removing their oppression.

The oppressed do indeed have a vital role to play and a contribution to make towards correcting the injustices of our society. When our Lord met the despised woman of Samaria at the well, he acknowledged her gift and thus affirmed her personhood when he asked her for a drink. And in the story he told about the 'good neighbour', it wasn't the Levite or the priest who showed good neighbourliness to the man who fell among thieves. It was the despised Samaritan and victim of discrimination who showed concern and took action in a situation that needed care and compassion. That story started with a lawyer asking: 'What shall I do to inherit eternal life?' It ended with Jesus telling the lawyer to take a lesson from the despised Samaritan: 'Go and do the same.'

* * *

And now a lawyer stood up and, to test him, asked, 'Master, what must I do to inherit eternal life?' He said to him, 'What is written in the Law? What is your reading of it?'

He replied, 'You must love the Lord your God with all your heart, with all your soul, with all your strength, and with all your mind, and your neighbour as yourself.' Jesus said to him, 'You have answered right, do this and life is yours.'

But the man was anxious to justify himself and said to Jesus, 'And who is my neighbour?' In answer Jesus said, 'A man was once on his way down from Jerusalem to Jericho and fell into the hands of bandits; they stripped him, beat him and then made off, leaving him half dead. Now a priest happened to be travelling down the same road, but when he saw the man, he passed by on the other side. In the same way a Levite who came to the place saw him, and passed by on the other side. But a Samaritan traveller who came on him was moved with compassion when he saw him. He went up to him and bandaged his wounds, pouring oil and wine on them. He then lifted him onto his own mount and took him to an inn and looked after him. Next day, he took out two denarii and handed them to the innkeeper and said, "Look after him, and on my way back I will make good any extra expense you have." Which of these three, do you think, proved himself a neighbour to the man who fell into the bandits' hands?' He replied, 'The one who showed pity towards him.' Jesus said to him, 'Go, and do the same yourself.' (Luke 10:25–37 NJB)

A PRAYER Lord, help me to go and do the same.

EQUALITY — 1

The minute I say I believe in equality then people say, 'Surely you don't mean that everybody is the same? Or that people ought to be the same? And that everybody ought to have the same wages and wear the same clothes?'

So I have to make it clear that I'm not talking about egalitarianism, which is about levelling everybody off in some mysterious way so that they are all treated exactly the same. What I actually believe in strongly is the value of people being different; and that's splendid and exciting and it makes life much more interesting.

A few years ago I had a marvellous sabbatical struggling with the whole idea of equality. In Scripture there are two themes which have to do with it. In Genesis 1 and 2 there are interesting things being said about the whole of mankind being made in the image of God.

So God created man in his own image, in the image of God he created him; male and female he created them. (Genesis 1:27)

That says something very important about equality of creation and equality of treatment as between male and female, and also about God in relation to his creation.

In the New Testament that theme is written out plainest of all in the great Pauline text in Galatians 3:28.

In Christ there is neither Jew nor Greek, neither slave nor free, there is neither male nor female; for you are all one in Christ Jesus.

Paul is talking in a context of baptism, but he is showing that baptism is reaffirming something which is also true in creation — the fundamental equality of men and women before God, of Jew and Greek before God, and of slave and free before God.

This theme is a very important one. In modern terms it is about what we would call fundamental equality in status before God. We are all equally the object of God's love. We are all equally the people for whom Christ died. We are all in that sense equal. But it has nothing to do with whether we all look alike, or are all equally clever, or all play the violin equally well — or any of the other idiotic things that people start saying when the subject of equality comes up.

The other biblical theme that helps us is the whole idea of fellowship in the New Testament. The Greek word for it is *koinonia*, which literally means 'common'; and it isn't a very long step from talking about our common life to talking about shared life, and the life that we have in common — or equally.

Then we start to realize that life itself is a gift and that life in the Spirit is a gift. So 'The grace of our Lord Jesus Christ, and the love of God, and the fellowship of the Holy Spirit' is about what we are given to enable us to belong to one another and to have this sense of what in modern terms we would call interdependence.

A PRAYER* Lord God, help me to love my neighbour as myself. Help me to realize our equality before you, who love us equally, and to whom we are equally precious.

Bishop Ronald Bowlby 3/Friday

EQUALITY — 2

The issue of equality is one which Christians have been very woolly about. I worked on it in my sabbatical because I believe it is a key issue. We have so often failed to work out its implications.

Christians have said: 'Well, you love God and you love your neighbour. And God loves everyone. So we must all be equal, mustn't we?' And that's about as far as it goes.

It doesn't begin to answer the modern arguments *against* equality, which are that if you say everybody is equal you destroy freedom, you destroy initiative and you destroy creativity — and what you produce is a sort of flat deadness.

The New Right thinking has majored in all this in the last fifteen to twenty years and in some ways their thinking has been correct. The other was flabby thinking — and the only un-flabby bit was rather Marxist.

What we need is a philosophy based on Christian thinking and belief which recognizes our basic equality before God. This fundamental equality must therefore be expressed in certain ways which will ensure that we always realize our interdependence as the children of God, made in his image.

When we get it right we shall never think that some of us are more important to God than others. But we shall know that we are all differently gifted. We shall use our gifts differently and be willing to share them.

Equality is a neglected area. Yet it is an extraordinarily important one. It is what the current debate between the political Right and the political Left is fundamentally about.

Many people in Britain today are very uneasy at the extent to which society is once again becoming polarized. The rich get richer and the poor get poorer. Ralph Darendorf has written about the emergence of a new under-class in America. Now he sees signs of a similar under-class emerging in Britain among the long-term unemployed (especially in the black community), who are alienated people with no stake in society and who then disrupt our cities out of frustration and despair.

Somehow we have got to recapture the middle ground between the extreme Left and the extreme Right. We need to have the confidence as Christians to say that if we do not attend to certain things there will be inevitable consequences. The sense of *koinonia* or fellowship both among Christians and within society will be destroyed.

As Christians we are not in the business of insisting that everyone has to have exactly the same treatment. It is that kind of 'equality' that has been under justified attack from the Right and also from others who see how it creates a grey, lifeless society.

We haven't all got to go to the same schools and all live in the same sized houses. But we have to say that there really are limits to the extent to which

STUDY GROUP MATERIAL

Second class citizens

1. Begin with the Coventry Cathedral Prayer.

2. What do you feel about people whose colour is different from yours? Do different colours arouse different feelings in you? If you can, share your feelings honestly — and then share what you think about your feelings (and about other people's feelings).

3. What do you feel about single homeless people who sleep on the streets? Do you think they are inferior people? Perhaps read out Ronald Bowlby's interview for Saturday, and discuss whether you could follow his suggestions about how to look at the problem.

PRAYING Sit in silence for a few moments, then read out the story of the Good Samaritan at the end of Wednesday. But as you listen, imagine that instead of lying at the side of the road wounded you are lying in the street with only a cardboard box for shelter.

people can have different levels of pay or education or openings, or whatever, because if you go too far you begin to destroy the fundamental equality which belongs to us as men and women made in the image of God. You destroy the common life (*koinonia*) which is not only in the body of Christ but which in some measure has got to be reflected in society. The church is a foretaste and a sign of the common life, but it is something for the world as well.

I think this is the way we have got to argue, because there are biblical roots to this. This can be the way through. We need a way through, because otherwise we are simply left with a few political slogans. What I have been doing is to start with the theology and then say, 'Right, now let's see what this means.'

A WAY FOR A GROUP TO PRAY As I get older I am more and more sure that one of the most important things that I have slowly, slowly been learning is to listen to other people's 'stories'. I suppose I am beginning to sound fashionable, and I don't mean to. I have been discovering it without using that language for a very long time.

When a group of Christians come together, sometimes one of the most useful things they can do for one another is simply to talk about what they have found most helpful in prayer, or why they became a Christian, or what is most difficult for them, or where is the shoe pinching.

You can vary the questions and come at the thing in different ways. And as you listen, what you will hear is the different ways in which the Holy Spirit has been dealing with people and gifting people. Without realizing it you will somehow begin to take into your own consciousness the sense that there is a real receiving of gifts in different ways, and that there is all this variety in the room where you are. Yet at the same time there is something common to it all which we share and which we can learn from, and that something is much greater than any particular natural gift.

Then perhaps that can move you into a different kind of prayer, by applying the same truth to some of the people you work with, in terms of how you intercede for them and hold them before the Lord.

* * *

Now Christ's body is yourselves, each of you with a part to play in the whole.
(1 Corinthians 12:27 NJB)

Not all flesh is alike, but there is one kind for men, another for animals, another for birds, and another for fish.

There are celestial bodies and there are terrestrial bodies; but the glory of the celestial is one, and the glory of the terrestrial is another.

There is one glory of the sun, and another glory of the moon, and another glory of the stars; for star differs from star in glory. (1 Cor. 15:39–41)

HOMELESS PEOPLE

Come now, you rich, weep and howl for the miseries that are coming upon you. Your riches have rotted and your garments are moth-eaten. Your gold and silver have rusted, and their rust will be evidence against you and will eat your flesh like fire.

You have laid up treasure for the last days. Behold, the wages of the labourers who mowed your fields, which you kept back by fraud, cry out; and the cries of the harvesters have reached the ears of the Lord of hosts.

You have lived on the earth in luxury and in pleasure; you have fattened your hearts in a day of slaughter. You have condemned, you have killed the righteous man; he does not resist you. (James 5:1–6)

There is nothing specific in the Bible about homelessness as such, but there is a clear stream of thinking about the way we treat the poor and the oppressed. It is very prominent in the Old Testament and in our Lord's teaching and in the letter of James.

An employer who holds back a farm-worker's wages and doesn't hand them over at the proper time is robbing him of his due, and God hears the cry of those who are being oppressed. Some of the homeless poor are oppressed, and helpless to do anything about it.

Elizabeth and I used to live next door to an old house in Croydon which was owned by a dreadful landlord. We were friends with the people who lived in the basement flat, and they had four little girls the same age as our children. The house was appallingly damp, with woefully inadequate plumbing, and the landlord would not repair anything.

The father of the little girls was an antique dealer, and he kept some of his stuff in the near-derelict garage. When the landlord discovered what he was doing he demanded a large sum of money for rent. When he refused to pay the landlord sent along a gang of men who bulldozed the garage to the ground, along with most of the stuff in it.

The same landlord bought up some houses in a beautiful crescent in Croydon, and before the Council could stop him he demolished two of the houses and completely spoiled the Crescent. That was the sort of man he was. All over Croydon there were people like our neighbours, who were being grossly overcharged and paying enormous rents for practically nothing. They were also being tricked on all sorts of legal or semi-legal grounds. It was those things that woke me up to the difficulties of the housing situation, and I started to get involved in it.

The problem of homelessness in London is appalling. It is a major social issue, and I believe that the churches ought to be particularly concerned about it. We say that we mind about family life, and that we mind about people having an environment in which their spiritual nature can grow and flourish. But if we do nothing about the homes they live in then we are ignoring a major factor in what blights people's life — especially the lives of children and young people.

What finally brought it all into focus for me as far as a knowledge of the subject was concerned was that I was invited to serve on the national housing enquiry chaired by the Duke of Edinburgh. The membership ranged from quite high-powered property tycoons and directors through to the Director of Shelter, and we were able to produce a unanimous report which offered a radical solution to get us out of the present mess, and a way forward over the next ten years. I think it has made a real contribution and had a good deal of influence. But we have still got a very long way to go.

PRAYING When I am listening to the intercessions in different churches it seems to me that people find it much easier to think about specific things to pray about concerning the church than they do concerning the world.

Perhaps we do not give people sufficient help in addressing the needs of the world and suggesting ways to pray that would waken up people's imaginations. We pray 'For the peace of the world. . .', 'for refugees. . .' — all those *huge* things. 'Let us pray for all the hungry people in the world' someone says, and I think, 'I'm not God, I can't do it. . .'

But supposing we also prayed, 'For Michael and Mandy, who have nowhere to live', or 'For wisdom to know what can be done about the homeless people in this district', or 'For *our* housing association'.

At the wedding in Cana of Galilee the wine ran out. Mary simply said to Jesus, 'They have no wine'. Pray now for just one person, or one couple whom you know, in the same sort of way. 'Lord, they have no home. . .'

Week 4

THE THIRD WORLD

OUR HALF OF THE WORLD is too fat and the other half of the world is too thin. So thin that millions of men, women and children die every year of starvation. But what on earth can we do? As individuals not very much. If we unite to take action then perhaps quite a lot.

In the USA Tony Campolo and some of his theological students set about trying to change an area of society in which they felt things were wrong. Some of the students worked in the Dominican Republic, in the shadow of the multi-national corporation Gulf & Western.

'It was exercising dramatic control over the life of the people', wrote Campolo, 'and taking over more and more of the land. We began to ask how could we get Gulf & Western to become an institution through which God could do good? We did not believe it was the enemy of God. Institutions are created by God to serve the people. So how can we take something like that and make it into an institution of change in society?'

They bought shares in the company and went to the meetings. They gave a biblical perspective to the things that were happening in the Dominican Republic and explained what they believed God wanted the company to do. So much of the land was being used by the company to grow sugar that there wasn't enough left for the people to grow food. Eventually the corporation agreed to lease back the land to the people and to commit $100 million to provide medical services. When we get together with other people it seems that we really can make things happen.

MENDING WHAT IS BROKEN

Here is my servant, whom I uphold, my chosen one in whom I delight. I have bestowed my spirit upon him, and he will make justice shine on the nations. He will not call out or lift his voice high, or make himself heard in the open street. He will not break a bruised reed or snuff out a smouldering wick; he will make justice shine on every race, never faltering, never breaking down; he will plant justice on earth, while coasts and islands wait for his teaching.

(Isaiah 42:1–4 NEB)

In a park I know there's a pond with some reeds growing in it. When they start growing they're green and supple and bendable, but late on in the year they go brown and dry and flop over. They are bruised reeds — and there's nothing much more useless and worthless than just one bruised reed. But Isaiah was writing about someone who wasn't going to see it that way — someone who wouldn't 'break a bruised reed. . .'

Reeds have a lot of things they can be used for. We can cut bundles of them out of the river and then thatch a roof with them. Or we can cut them down and cut holes in them and make music with them. . . And if we don't carve one of them right the first time we can throw it away and try again. There are so many of them that they're disposable — like people, perhaps?

When I was feeling very sad once I heard someone talking about a reed that was a reed to make music with. He was preaching a sermon about this saying of Isaiah — that the servant of God is somebody who won't break a bruised reed.

He told us to imagine that the reed was a musical pipe which had got damaged. Either someone had been careless and dropped it. Or else somehow it had done something it shouldn't, and managed to get itself on to the edge of its shelf and fallen off — and got damaged that way. But it didn't make any difference whether it was its own fault or somebody else's fault. . . because the heart of the story was what this strange servant of God did with the bruised reed.

What he didn't do was to pick it up and break it in two and then throw it away. He did something else. He took it into his hands and bound it up and mended it. Then he put it to his mouth and blew through it, and the sound that he could play on it now was sweeter and truer than it had been before.

Reeds grow in rivers and ponds all over the world, and one of the reeds in Palestine grows ten feet high. They put a reed like that once into the hands of Jesus, just before they took him out to be crucified. They took his clothes off and dressed him up in a scarlet robe, and then stuck a crown on his head that they'd made out of thorns. The reed that they had given him was his sceptre.

Before they took Jesus out to crucify him they took the reed out of his hand and used it to hit him on the head with. When he was on the cross, he cried out those terrible words of dereliction, 'My God, my God, why hast thou forsaken me. . .?' And they took another reed, and put a sponge on the end of it soaked in sour wine, and they hoisted it up to him, so that he could suck the wine out of the sponge. Then he cried out again, and then he died.

A PRAYER Lord, sometimes we're like reeds that have got bruised and damaged. Take us into your hands and mend us — you who are the maker and mender of human souls. Then anoint us with your Spirit, and help us to do for other hurt and broken people what you have done for us.

Dr Pauline Cutting 4/Monday

REFUGEES

Pauline Cutting has been described as a reluctant heroine. She worked as a doctor in a Palestinian refugee camp when it was under siege. I asked her what normal conditions were like in such a camp.

Life in a refugee camp is very hard. There are all sorts of physical hardships. Difficult daily living, the getting of water, the providing of food.

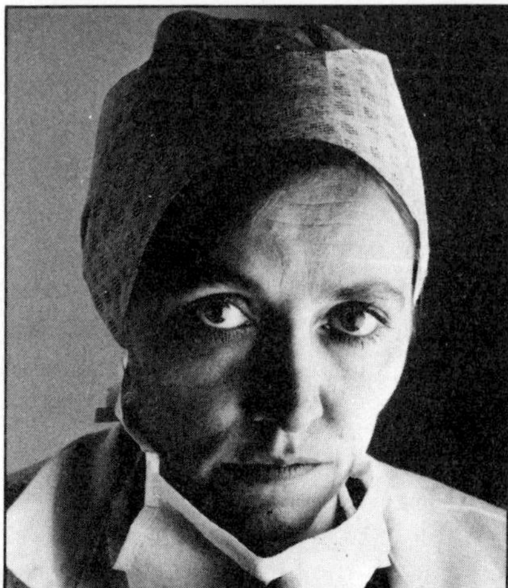

Dr Pauline Cutting

Dr Pauline Cutting has been described as a reluctant heroine. She works for Medical Aid for Palestine, and came into the public eye when she worked in a Palestinian refugee camp which was under siege. She recently got engaged to a Dutchman who also worked in the camp, and she spends a lot of time in Holland.

People are extremely crowded and they suffer the diseases and the health consequences of overcrowding, poverty and enforced exile.

But I think it is the enforced exile which affects them more deeply than anything else. They have an overriding, burning desire to return to their own homes — the homes that they either fled from or from which they were forced out. Even the Palestinians that I have spoken to who are materially well off, and who don't live in the refugee camps, have just the same longing to go home. They haven't given up their nationality and their identity. Those things don't just dissolve with time.

I think it was George Bernard Shaw who said that, 'If you take away a person's nationhood then they will strive through all sorts of difficulty, through thick and thin, to regain it — and nothing will stand in the way of that.'

What would you feel like if you had been turned out of your country?

I think I would feel very bitter indeed. And I would want to go home. I hadn't realized that they had been turned out. It was only when I sat and talked to people about what had happened to them that I found out. And having lived with them and worked with them in hard times it made it even more poignant.

Can you say what happened in Palestine?

The Jews were being persecuted in the world, especially in Europe, and the persecution had gone on for a long time. It wasn't just in the second world war. Well before that. The Zionists introduced the idea of a Jewish state, and that was supported originally by the British in the Balfour Declaration of 1917, which suggested a Jewish Homeland, and ultimately supported by the United Nations.

So in 1947 Palestine was partitioned. That was never agreed to by the Palestinian Arabs who were living there — hardly surprisingly. Then in 1948 there was a war in which the Zionists captured much larger areas of Palestine, and during that war many of the Palestinians either fled because they feared for their lives or were expelled by the Zionists. That was the biggest exodus of Palestinians. They went to Lebanon, to Egypt, to Jordan and to Syria. Some have scattered all over the world. But mostly they are there, and most of those who have remained live in the refugee camps provided by the United Nations.

They were never allowed to return by the new Israeli government and so they stayed there. Then in 1967 there was another war in which what remained of the original land of British Mandated Palestine was captured by the Israelis and that is what we now refer to as the Occupied Territories, because they are not governed by the same laws as Israel but by a military occupation. During that war more Palestinians left or were expelled and those who left were never allowed to go back. They have remained outside as refugees.

So they stand for all refugees, don't they?

Yes. It is very similar. Many other refugee communities are born not by the creation of a new state but as the result of armed conflict. And in Africa the plight of the refugees in many areas is complicated even more by armed conflict.

If a group of people said to you, 'We feel so helpless when we look at the refugee problem — is there anything we can do at all?', what would you say to them? Is it just physical help in the form of money that they can give?

No. We have been more concerned with physical aid in terms of medical aid. But I feel that other people have a part to play. My own feeling is that the only way to end the conflict is that groups concerned must come together for a negotiated peaceful settlement which will involve some sort of sharing. Therefore I think that any groups who are brought together to discuss those issues can only help to contribute to the ultimate peace of the region. That will raise awareness and then perhaps provide a platform for ideas that might lead to a settlement.

* * *

Now, people of Israel, listen to what the Lord your God demands of you: Worship the Lord and do all that he commands. Love him, serve him with all your heart, and obey all his laws. I am giving them to you today for your benefit. To the Lord belong even the highest heavens; the earth is his also, and everything on it. But the Lord's love for your ancestors was so strong that he chose you instead of any other people, and you are still his chosen people. So then, from now on be obedient to the Lord and stop being stubborn. The Lord your God. . . makes sure that orphans and widows are treated fairly; he loves the foreigners who live with our people, and gives them food and clothes. So then, show love for those foreigners, because you were once foreigners in Egypt. (Deuteronomy 10:12–19 GNB)

A PRAYER* O God our Father, the God of Abraham, of Isaac and of Jacob, it says that we Christians too are 'a chosen race, a holy nation, God's own people'. Help us to imagine what it would be like to be refugees — turned out of our own country. Help us to do for them what we would like them to do for us if things were the other way round.

N.B. The Bible passage was selected by the Editor — NOT Pauline Cutting

PRAYING THE KINGDOM

One of Charles Elliott's best-selling books is *Praying the Kingdom*, so I began our interview by asking him what he thought the kingdom was and how we were to pray for it.

You can't define the kingdom. That's the whole point. It is God's kingdom and not ours, and I am very suspicious of attempts to define it either in political terms or social terms or spiritual terms. Yet I think that most people who go round with their inner eyes open see signs of it in all kinds of unlikely places.

I have just come back from a workshop in Leeds where people have been working on inner city justice issues and I was very conscious that they are signs of the kingdom. Later this month my wife will be running a retreat for people in the Peace Movement. So she will be in touch with people who, if you like to put it that way, are 'signs of the kingdom'.

The exciting thing is that wherever one goes one sees what I call 'lighthouse people', who are signs that 'the kingdom is very close to us'.

We pray for the kingdom as Jesus prayed for it. We pray that the kingdom will come. We pray that we will be sensitive to where it is already breaking in — and recognize that it is very near to us. We pray that we will be part of the process of its breaking in. The kingdom is breaking in wherever people are freed from fear and greed and a lust for the wrong sort of security. It is breaking in wherever people are enabled to become more what God created us to be, which is to be free enough to worship him and praise him and live in real community with one another.

* * *

One of the rulers put this question to him, 'Good Master, what shall I do to inherit eternal life?' Jesus said to him, 'Why do you call me good? No one is good but God alone. You know the commandments: You shall not commit adultery; You shall not kill; You shall not steal; You shall not give false witness; Honour your father and your mother.' He replied, 'I have kept all these since my earliest days.' And when Jesus heard this he said, 'There is still one thing you lack. Sell everything you own and distribute the money to the poor, and you will have treasure in heaven; then come, follow me.' But when he heard this he was overcome with sadness, for he was very rich.

Jesus looked at him and said, 'How hard it is for those who have riches to make their way into the kingdom of God! Yes, it is easier for a camel to pass through the eye of a needle than for someone rich to enter the kingdom of God.' Those who were listening said, 'In that case, who can be saved?' He replied, 'Things that are impossible by human resources, are possible for God.'

The Revd Prebendary Charles Elliott

Charles Elliott is a theologian and an economist. He has taught in universities in Britain and Africa; spent five years in Zambia; worked for three years in Geneva with Sodepax, a joint RC/WCC committee on society, development and peace; and has been a special advisor to the House of Commons Select Committee on Overseas Development. He was Director of Christian Aid. He is the author of award-winning books on prayer. He and his wife Hilary have three adult sons.

But Peter said, 'Look, we left all we had to follow you.' He said to them, 'In truth I tell you, there is no one who has left house, wife, brothers, parents or children for the sake of the kingdom of God who will not receive many times as much in this present age and, in the world to come, eternal life.'

(Luke 18:18–30 NJB)

A PRAYER

Our Father in heaven,
Hallowed be your name.
Your kingdom come,
Your will be done on earth. . .

Prebendary Charles Elliott — 4/Wednesday

WHAT CAN I DO?

When we are looking at the problems of the third world we have got to be sensitive to the people who live in it. We have got to be aware of their situation. They have got to go on struggling with the issues where *they* are, not where we are. But there are things we can do to help ourselves to understand.

First, we mustn't just think in terms of the third world 'out there'. The third world — or the fourth world — is often on our own doorstep, and it is the people who are on the underside of our own society. It is often when we are in touch with that fourth world on our own doorstep that we become more sensitive to the issues of the third world out there.

Second, we must forget about giving and learn to receive. It is only when we have learned to receive from the fourth world, or the third world, that we shall actually be able to give.

It always worries me that the immediate Christian response is, 'What can I give?' The answer is, 'Nothing. Be like the Jew in the story of the Good Samaritan and learn to receive. Once you've learned to receive then you'll learn to give.'

Third, we must try to look at the facts behind the facts. When you take seriously what some people (particularly in the Roman Catholic Church) call 'Social Analysis' that will lead you to question your political choices, your lifestyle choices, and maybe even your career choices. It isn't adequate any longer to say, 'All right, I'll have a coffee morning and raise £1,000 for Tear Fund.' If it stops at that, that's a cop out and it has to be named as a cop out. We have got to be asking questions about the structures of our society.

Why are there now more homeless people in London than there have ever been in this century?

Why is unemployment so high?

Why are poor countries being paid less and less (in terms of import purchasing power) for the things they sell us?

Those are the kinds of questions we have to ask rather than assume that the present structures of our society are Acts of God.

If people ask, 'What can I do to be saved?', I don't want to be negotiated into saying: 'These are the kinds of things you should be doing.' People have to take responsibility for themselves and for their own situation. It isn't adequate to lie on one's back with one's paws in the air. It is a question of struggling with where you are in life — your own situation and that of your immediate community — and then taking responsibility.

* * *

If you want to know what God wants you to do, ask him, and he will gladly tell you, for he is always ready to give a bountiful supply of wisdom to all those who ask him; he will not resent it. But when you ask him, be sure that you really expect him to tell you, for a doubtful mind will be as unsettled as a wave of the sea that is driven and tossed by the wind; and every decision you then make will be uncertain, as you turn first this way, and then that. If you don't ask with faith, don't expect the Lord to give you any solid answer.

(James 1:5–8 The Living Bible)

A PRAYER* Lord God, give us wisdom. Help us to ask the right questions and to find out the right answers. Help us to struggle with the issues that face us, and then to take responsibility and take the right action.

AN OVERABUNDANT GENEROSITY

When I was working in Africa there was a young man in my little congregation whose name was Tembo. He was practically uneducated. But one day, when I was sitting on his doorstep, he taught me a profound theological truth. To understand the truth you have to know a little of the language.

There is a marvellous word in the Chinyanja language. *Maningi*. It means 'too much; an overabundance; a surplus; a great welling up'. As we were sitting there Tembo suddenly said to me, 'Ah, we have a *maningi* God. . .' That's a phrase which has lived with me for a very long time. The image of God as someone who is 'too much', who is overabundantly generous, who gives of an enormous richness.

For me that has opened up a whole series of meditative doors. Here was a young man from a remote part of Zambia, almost totally uneducated, and yet he could see to the heart of the loving generosity of God in a way that I could never begin to do.

Those of us who have gone through the business of learning to receive and be in touch with people in the third world and on the underside of our own community are finding that it brings our prayer alive in a quite startling way. It revolutionizes it.

For me the core of praying the kingdom is the engagement of my own prayer life, and that of my fellow Christians, with the major issues of today, and with the structural issues. But it is not just about mobilizing social and political action or the investigation of alternatives, although it *is* about both those. It is actually to confront the powers and principalities that hold this present world in bondage at the deepest level of the spirit. That is what it is all about.

Unless we are prepared to engage those powers at the deepest spiritual and psychological level, both in ourselves and in our community, then we are avoiding the real issue.

An extract from PRAYING THE KINGDOM, Towards a Political Spirituality:

. . . For the Israelite, at its best the law was a working out of what loving kindness means in everyday relationships.

You must not pervert justice in dealing with a stranger or an orphan, nor take a widow's garment in pledge. Remember that you were a slave in Egypt and that Yahweh your God redeemed you from there. That is why I lay this charge on you.

When reaping the harvest in your field, if you have overlooked a sheaf in that field, do not go back for it. Leave it for the stranger, the orphan and the widow, so that Yahweh your God may bless you in all your undertakings.

When you beat your olive trees you must not go over the branches twice. Let anything left be for the stranger, the orphan and the widow.

When you harvest your vineyard you must not pick it over a second time. Let anything left be for the stranger, the orphan and the widow.

Remember that you were a slave in the land of Egypt. That is why I lay this charge on you. (Deuteronomy 24:17–22)

Read that passage two or three more times — slowly. Remember that the key thing about the widow, the orphan and the stranger is that they had no claim to land of their own. They were therefore symbols of those who could expect nothing as of right: exactly parallel with the legal, ethical and religious condition of Israel with respect to Yahweh. Israel as a people had to depend on Yahweh's love; nothing more. They had no *claim* on it. The widow, the orphan and the stranger had no *claim* on society. As Yahweh had redeemed

STUDY GROUP MATERIAL

The Third World

1. Begin with the Coventry Cathedral Prayer.

2. Perhaps read out Charles Elliott's first interview about the kingdom of God. Is this something that you think about very much? When you pray in the Lord's Prayer 'Thy kingdom come. . .', what do you hope will happen?

2. Perhaps read out Charles Elliott's second interview. In your area, where is the fourth world? What does it make you feel?

3. What do you think and feel about giving aid to other countries? Are you prepared to find out the facts about the sort of aid we are giving, and whether it is what will really help the country concerned?

PRAYING Be still for a few moments in silence. Then read out Luke 18:18–30 at the end of Charles Elliott's first interview.

Then, very slowly, pray the Lord's Prayer out loud, with quite long pauses between the phrases.

Israel, so now the people must celebrate that liberation by showing the same loving generosity to those who had no claim on them.

It is this ethic that we need to let come alive in us. It is the ethic that I shall call, after Jean Vanier, the ethic of gratuity. That is a word that many people find difficult. 'To people in my station in life', said a wealthy but well-meaning friend, 'gratuity is what you give the boot boy'. Perhaps, but in its original, deeper meaning gratuity was the virtue of overwhelming love expressing itself in almost excessive generosity. A Parsee friend of mine had a grandmother who was very, very rich. Living in Karachi in the last years of the last century, she was inevitably surrounded by poor people who hoped for the odd crumbs that might fall from her table. A deeply religious woman, she was so generous that her family easily foresaw the early disappearance of the family fortune. They stopped her carrying money so she couldn't give it away. They ensured that no poor person was allowed to enter the house so she wouldn't give away the precious furniture and priceless ornaments. . .

One day a toothless old woman somehow managed to wheedle her way into the drawing room. 'A sari, a sari,' she cried. . . 'This rag is all I have.' 'I cannot give you a sari,' the lady of the house explained, 'for they have locked all the cupboards. But if you don't mind washing this. . .' and she took off the richly decorated silk sari she was wearing and presented it to the old woman. . .

Such is gratuity. . .

To bring about the notion of gratuity — for it is an ethic that applies to communities and nations as well as individuals — here is an exercise you might like to try with the passage from Deuteronomy in mind.

IMAGINE you are a small farmer, growing corn. Yours is a family farm, just large enough to keep you and your two sons. It is a hard life and, as agricultural policy and technology increasingly favour the larger farmer, it is getting harder. Just before harvest, there is a serious disaster in another part of the country, and an aid agency asks all farmers to give one ton of corn in five to help feed those at risk. You have to decide how you will respond to that request.

What would enable you to respond joyfully and cheerfully? A law, passed by the government, demanding an extra tax of 20 per cent of your production? A direct request from the people concerned? Television pictures of starving children?. . . Or the heart-knowledge of being loved so freely and generously that a joyful response is the only one available to you?

I have not been able to include quite all this meditation, but there is

enough here to work on. Charles Elliott's book contains other meditations and ways to pray the kingdom, just as insightful and helpful as this one.

The Revd Brian Branche 4/Friday

LUNCH AND LOOS

One of the worst things about having no work and no money was boredom. There was nothing to do all day apart from walking the streets. There was nowhere to go. If I had gone to the library all day that would have been cheating. I did go, because I was trying to live a Benedictine rule of work, study and prayer. My prayer was fixed in the morning, midday and evening, although it took a lot of discipline. My study was going into the library for an hour in the afternoon.

That helped me to realize how important public buildings are. The library was one of the free places you could go and sit and be warm. If everything is private enterprise and you've got no money, you are out in the streets and in the cold.

If you have been smelly and had lice would they have let you sit in the library or would they have given you the push?

I don't know. The possibility is always there that if you are undesirable you will be told to move. But my idea wasn't to be scruffy. It was to keep myself as well as I could.

But you realize how important loos are. My greatest prayer was, 'Lord, where's the nearest loo?' Then when you find one and it's the sort you have to pay for you have to start counting. Is it worth 10p or do you find a quiet corner in the street and use the 10p towards a cup of tea?

My whole way of thinking was being re-ordered. In order to survive I had to learn to live again. I found myself looking to see where was the cheapest cup of tea, where was the cheapest slice of toast? And I would shop until I found the cheapest. I'd be adding up and counting, and if something was a penny cheaper it would be worth walking half a mile to get there.

The hostel cost me £41 for the week and that was good value. We got breakfast and supper except on Saturday and Sunday when we just had breakfast. The first weekend I was there I went the whole time on just my breakfast. If I had bought supper and lunch out it would have cost me £6 and I would only have had £2 to last the rest of the week.

The following week I looked to see what the others were doing, and what they did was to take a fistful of bread and butter on Saturday morning from the breakfast. So I did the same, and my Saturday and Sunday lunch and evening meal was bread and butter.

I had my own room, but the toilets were shared. Because I was living with unemployed people I had to get used to their habits. I'd go to the toilet and find someone had messed on the pan. People who are angry start to lose respect for things, and the unemployed and the underprivileged are angry. So everything deteriorates and your whole life deteriorates. You feel hopeless.

I locked myself in my room for three days and I cried. I went back to being a child and I broke down. In my most vulnerable situation I encountered myself. I couldn't suppress the fears that were inside me and I was a junkie being withdrawn. I didn't have the things that would suppress the fears. I couldn't go and read, or go and do something useful. Those things would have stopped me from going into the deep. 'Out of the deep it is that I cry to you, Lord.' But most of us don't cry out from the deep. We cry out from the shallow end.

An extract from Brian's diary
Dear God, I don't want ever to be poor or underprivileged.

We have a fundamental need to have control over our destiny — which actually says something about the anger in people who are not in a position to alter their circumstances. We get very angry when we are unable to do so and that's what I'm feeling now. . . It is the kind of feeling we face when we are bereft — when we find out how powerless we are.

All the cosmetics cannot cover up the pain and even God seems unable to come to my aid. 'My God, my God, why hast thou forsaken me. . .'

* * *

Save me, O God!
    For the waters have come up to my neck.
I sink in deep mire,
    where there is no foothold;
I have come into deep waters,
    and the flood sweeps over me.
I am weary with my crying;
    my throat is parched.
My eyes grow dim
    with waiting for my God.

(Psalm 69:1–3)

A PRAYER* Lord God, thank you for Sunday dinner — for roast lamb and roast potatoes and green peas and gravy and for apple pie and. . .

cream. Thank you for hot water and baths and warm, comforting towels. Thank you for WCs that are only used by me and my family and friends.

But what about the people who haven't got those things? Is there anything that you want me to do?

Dame Peggy Fenner, MP 4/Saturday

A POLITICAL CAMPAIGN

All political parties (and all churches!) are imperfect, because all human beings are imperfect and if we refuse to support what is not totally perfect we shall never get involved in anything at all. Political action is one way to change the world, and slavery would never have been abolished if Wilberforce had refused to fight. Perhaps as Christians we need to support any initiative that helps the poor.

In the spring of 1988 the Council of Europe began an international campaign about the interdependence of Europe and the Third World. Dame Peggy Fenner invited me to tea in the House of Commons and told me what the campaign was trying to do.

The proper title is the European Campaign on North-South Interdependence and Solidarity — and North-South is shorthand for the more affluent countries and the less affluent countries. We are saying that we should improve our behaviour to the Third World.

It is really a campaign for Christians and for Christian behaviour. We want to inform people and get the support of all the people in the 21 countries of the Council of Europe, because we consider that political action is best taken if the people are pressing their governments to take it.

We are saying that we must help the people who need our help and who have a very low standard of living. But we are not just presenting it by saying that this is the right way to behave to people who are deprived. It is also enlightened self-interest, because it is very necessary that the less well off countries of the world should improve their standard of living and have improved economies. Then they can buy goods and equipment from the more affluent countries. At the moment whole sections of the world are so poor that they cannot buy the things that are available to enrich their lives and improve their living.

We are saying that the more affluent countries need to consider the debt of the Third World and write it off — just as some commercial banks in Britain

Dame Peggy Fenner, MP

Peggy Fenner is the MP for Medway. She is married to Bernard and they have one daughter and two grandchildren. Before she became an MP she was active for seventeen years in local government. She was a junior minister at MAFF for seven years and she likes people, reading, travelling and cooking.

have written off their Third World debts, and Britain has been introducing her own initiative into the International Monetary Fund and the World Bank to help the process. We have written off the aid debts of 22 of the poorest countries at a cost of just under £1,000 million, and this is a policy that we have continued to promote among the countries of the world in connection with the debt of the Third World.

One aim of this Campaign is to show people what a small world it is and how interdependent we are. We want to improve living for people throughout the world. This is a common task in which we all have to share and it is our Christian duty to do this.

If anyone wants to know more about all this they can write to Patricia Shepheard, c/o CWDE, Regent's College, London NW1 4NS or to the Information Department, Council of Europe, BP 431 R6 F-67006 Strasbourg CEDEX.

* * *

Teach the king to judge with your righteousness, O God; share with him your own justice, so that he will rule over your people with justice and govern the oppressed with righteousness.

May the land enjoy prosperity; may it experience righteousness. May the king judge the poor fairly; may he help the needy and defeat their oppressors. . .

May the king be like rain on the fields, like showers falling on the land. . .

He rescues the poor who call to him, and those who are needy and neglected. He has pity on the weak and poor; he saves the lives of those in need. He rescues them from oppression and violence; their lives are precious to him. (Psalm 72:1–4, 6, 12–14 GNB)

A BLESSING *prayed by Martin Luther King for his congregation in Montgomery when he left them to spend all his time in political action:*

And now unto him who is able to keep us from falling
and lift us from the dark valley of despair to the bright mountain of hope,
from the midnight of desperation to the daybreak of joy;
to him be power and authority, for ever and ever.

Father, Forgive. . .

The hatred which divides nation from nation
race from race, class from class,
Father, forgive.
The covetous desires of men and nations
to possess what is not their own,
Father, forgive.
The greed which exploits the labours of men,
and lays waste the earth,
Father, forgive.
Our envy of the welfare and happiness of others,
Father, forgive.
Our indifference to the plight of the homeless
and the refugee,
Father, forgive.
The lust which uses for ignoble ends
the bodies of men and women,
Father, forgive.
The pride which leds to trust in ourselves
and not in God,
Father, forgive.

Week 5

PEACE AND JUSTICE

WHEN I WAS THINKING what pictures would best illustrate all the sections of *My World* the only one that came into my mind for this section on Peace and Justice was the statue on top of the Old Bailey of a woman with scales in her hand. But that didn't seem quite right, until the other day I actually saw the statue on television. Then it did seem right, because I had never realized that the scales which she held in one hand were matched by the sword which she held in her other hand. Sometimes peace and justice can only be achieved by fighting for them.

Peace and justice are not just about weighing things up and giving verdicts. They are about being fair to people and about everything being in harmony, like a great symphony played without one wrong note. They are about no one being left out in the cold, and about everyone being loved and treated as they ought to be and as they want to be. The way to know if it's right from the receiving end is to attend to the words in the Sermon on the Mount: 'So whatever you wish that men would do to you, do so to them. . .' If that was just what was wanted, then it was right. . .

If we are hungry we shall want someone to feed us; if we are thirsty we shall want someone to give us a drink; and if we are homeless we shall want someone to find us a home. And we shan't want them to do those things looking down their noses at us. We shall want them to happen with love and respect, given with a smiling face and kind eyes.

A PLACE FOR GOD

For unto us a child is born, unto us a son is given; and the government shall be upon his shoulder: and his name shall be called Wonderful, Counsellor, The mighty God, The everlasting Father, The Prince of Peace. Of the increase of his government and peace there shall be no end, upon the throne of David, and upon his kingdom, to order it, and to establish it with judgement and with justice from henceforth even for ever. The zeal of the Lord of hosts will perform this. (Isaiah 9:6–7)

A tiny, unborn baby growing inside his mother — and growing there because Mary had said 'Yes' to God and permitted it. She had made herself a place for God to be born in:

'Behold, the handmaid of the Lord. Be it unto me according to your word.'

Then there was a tiny, newborn baby, lying in a manger. Lying there because the innkeeper had given him a place to be born in. Not the best place in the house. But it was a place — a space — to lay a newborn baby in the hay of a manger, wrapped in swaddling clothes.

There is nothing frightening about a baby. It isn't going to overpower people. The baby is helpless — and if no one will help it to grow and to live then it won't grow and it won't live.

Helpless. Powerless. Asking for a space to be born in. Asking for room. Asking for a place — the baby that was born at Bethlehem. But only helpless and powerless when he was a baby and when he was nailed on the cross outside Jerusalem.

This one is also 'The mighty God, the everlasting Father, the Prince of Peace. . .' He is 'the image of the invisible God, the first born of all creation', and 'for him all things were created, in heaven and on earth, visible and invisible, whether thrones or dominions or principalities or authorities — all things were created through him and for him. He is before all things, and in him all things hold together' (Colossians 1:15–17).

'Born to raise the sons of earth,
Born to give them second birth'

. . . and the daughters of earth too. When the baby grew up to manhood he had a quite a different attitude to the daughters of earth than the other sons of earth had. But then this man wasn't just a son of earth. He was the Son of God. Truly God and truly man.

'Born to give them a second birth' — if they want one. If they want a relationship with God the Father that they have never had before. A new life, and a whole new start.

But they had better be sure who it is that they are letting in and making a place for.

> I saw a stable, low and very bare,
> A little child in a manger.
> The oxen knew him, had him in their care.
> To men he was a stranger.
> The safety of the world was lying there,
> And the world's danger.
>
> (Mary Elizabeth Coleridge)

Archbishop John Habgood 5/Monday

PEACE

I asked the Archbishop of York to talk to me about peace and justice and he said that those two themes are brought very close together by the prophet Jeremiah. Jeremiah writes of everyone from the least to the greatest practising deceit, 'dressing the wounds of God's people lightly', and saying 'Peace, peace' when there is no peace.

There is a spurious kind of peace, which conceals a great deal of pain and grief. There are remedies which are supposed to be remedies, but they do not heal and they do not get down to the root of the problem.

The people who are concerned about peace and justice in our day point to an ideal of peace expressed within the scriptures. It is a vision of ultimate harmony. In practical terms we have to recognize that life will always be a matter of compromise and of doing the best we can in unpropitious circumstances. But nevertheless there must be this ultimate vision of harmony in God. Justice is an integral part of that harmony, because in an unjust world there can be no true peace.

Dr Habgood works in the World Council of Churches, where peace and justice are major themes to which everyone devotes a great deal of attention. But what is not often admitted is that peace and justice are frequently in conflict. How much injustice can be tolerated in the cause of peace? If there is to be peace in many of the warring areas in our world today, some people are going to have to swallow their pride. Or perhaps they will say, 'We'll put up with injustice for the time being in the interests of peace'.

This is what happened in Northern Ireland. For a long time there was a peace there which was no peace, because deep feelings of resentment were building up beneath the surface among those who had had an unfair deal.

I asked Dr Habgood to tell me about the biblical concept of peace, which I understood was a far bigger thing than just the absence of war. 'It is indeed', he said. 'It is such a large concept that it can virtually include our whole relationship with God. I suppose that our words "harmony" and "completeness" come nearest to it. It is about everything finding its true fulfilment in God and in relation to one another in a totally harmonious way. Therefore peace is determined by our relationship with God, an obedience to and oneness with the will of God which then spreads out into every relationship in life and to the whole natural order.'

The trouble is, as Dr Habgood pointed out, that when we start trying to translate this into practical terms we have to accept some things which are a great deal less than the ideal. The biblical concept of peace may be a far bigger thing than the absence of war, but in a warring world the latter would still be a great improvement on our present lack of peace.

* * *

'The wise men shall be put to shame, they shall be dismayed and taken; lo, they have rejected the word of the Lord, and what wisdom is in them? Therefore I will give their wives to others and their fields to conquerors, because from the least to the greatest every one is greedy for unjust gain; from prophet to priest every one deals falsely. They have healed the wound of my people lightly, saying, "Peace, peace," when there is no peace.'

(Jeremiah 8:9–11)

The Archbishop of York

John Habgood was formerly a scientist, teaching and researching in Cambridge. He was Bishop of Durham for ten years and has written several books: *Religion and Science; A Working Faith; Church and Nation in a Secular Age* and (forthcoming) *Confessions of a Conservative Liberal*. He is married to Rosalie and they have two sons, two daughters, two dogs and two cats. He is interested in almost everything (except sport). . .travel, painting, music, DIY, poetry, etc.

A SIMPLE PRAYER

Lord, make me an instrument of your peace.
Where there is hatred . . . let me sow love.
Where there is injury . . . pardon.
Where there is discord . . . unity.
Where there is doubt . . . faith.
Where there is error . . . truth.
Where there is despair . . . hope.
Where there is sadness . . . joy.
Where there is darkness . . . light.
(attributed to St Francis of Assisi)

Archbishop John Habgood 5/Tuesday

JUSTICE

I asked the Archbishop to define the biblical word 'justice' (*mishpat*) and he told me that it was very difficult to give a general definition. The experience of most people is that it is much easier to recognize injustice than to say in advance what positive justice would actually be like.

People know very well when they have been treated *un*-fairly. If we are looking for an ideal of a just society then the concept of fairness, or equal opportunity, or equality in some other sense, can all be helpful. But in practice it is best to look at particular situations and work out what particular injustices need to be remedied. Then as a result of specific action we see what improvements have been made towards a fairer society.

I then asked Dr Habgood what he thought a small group of people might be able to do to help if they got together. His answer was that the first thing is always to try to understand. We need to inform our consciences about what is happening in different parts of the world. When we see things happening that are unjust, we shall find ourselves strongly motivated to take some action.

One of the useful things that the media have done is simply to expose things that are happening so that we can see what the issues are. They show us a mother struggling to bring up her baby in one room, with a leaking roof and paper peeling off the ceiling. Then, because we have seen it, we know better what it is like to live in some appalling slum. They show us a man being knocked down on to the ground by a blow across his face from a rifle — and we begin to comprehend just a little of what it must be like to live under some oppressive regime.

That's the first step: to inform our consciences about what is happening. The second step is much more difficult. We must consult with the people who are suffering the injustice and let them dictate the agenda. So often people who have had their consciences aroused say, 'We must do something', and they go off and do what *they* think is right, and in fact make the situation much worse.

Dr Habgood told me how they are getting it right in one of the unemployment black spots in Middlesborough. One of the responses over many years to the very high rates of unemployment has been to say, 'Let us learn from the unemployed themselves what this is like, and how they can make the most of their condition.'

An organization called IMPASSE, which has operated on Teeside for ten

STUDY GROUP MATERIAL

Peace and Justice

1. Begin with the Coventry Cathedral Prayer.

2. In a few moments of silence, let everybody think of an incident in their past life in which they felt they were treated unfairly. Then those who are willing can share the incident and share their feelings.

3. Read out Peter Selby's interview for Saturday. How do you feel about having enough space for yourself? Discuss the idea of the two actors both filling all the stage.

PRAYING Sit in silence for a few moments and then read out the passage from Ezekiel in the Archbishop of York's Tuesday interview. Think about the poor and homeless in the world. . . If in a sense they are lost and hungry sheep, and God is the divine shepherd, imagine what it would be like for them to be found and fed. Imagine yourself as an under-shepherd doing that work.

Perhaps use the Archbishop's way of praying at the end of Tuesday, choosing a situation in the world that you are particularly concerned about to lay before God like Hezekiah's letter.

Finish with the prayer at the end of Monday's interview.

years, has enabled many unemployed people to find a whole new way of living by being encouraged to work through their problems together.

* * *

'Thus says the Lord God: Ho, shepherds of Israel who have been feeding yourselves! Should not shepherds feed the sheep? You eat the fat, you clothe yourselves with the wool, you slaughter the fatlings; but you do not feed the sheep.

'The weak you have not strengthened, the sick you have not healed, the crippled you have not bound up, the strayed you have not brought back, the lost you have not sought, and with force and harshness you have ruled them. . . My sheep were scattered over all the face of the earth, with none to search or seek for them. . .

'I myself will be the shepherd of my sheep, and I will make them lie down, says the Lord God. I will seek the lost, and I will bring back the strayed, and I will bind up the crippled, and I will strengthen the weak, and the fat and the strong I will watch over; I will feed them in justice.' (Ezekiel 34:2–6, 15–16)

A WAY TO PRAY The Archbishop's way of praying for a group of people, or for an individual, is to spread the situation out before the Lord — just as Hezekiah did with his letter from the King of Assyria.

Hezekiah received the letter from the hand of the messengers, and read it; and Hezekiah went up to the house of the Lord, and spread it before the Lord. And Hezekiah prayed before the Lord. . . (2 Kings 19:14–15)

The right way to pray in the face of injustice is not to think through a solution and then dictate it to God, telling him what to do. The right way is simply to tell God what the situation is, and to acknowledge our own powerlessness and blindness. Then we ask that we and others may be responsive to the will of God. Some of the things that we then think of doing may seem trivial given the enormous size of the problems — but if we have really felt our own powerlessness and weakness God will give us the courage to go and do them.

> 'My power is made perfect in weakness. . .'
> (2 Corinthians 12:9)

Lord Murray 5/Wednesday

WHAT'S WORK?

We have got to get a new definition of what we mean by work. One of the lessons of the parable of the vineyard is that even if you can't find work you still have the right to the same standards of living as the people who have been fortunate enough to find work.

One definition is that work is something that you don't like doing so you have to get paid for it, while leisure is what you like doing so much that you don't expect to be paid. Like a man lying under his car on a Saturday morning doing his tappets: he's dripping with oil and enormously enjoying himself, so when he gets out from under his car he doesn't expect anybody to hand him a £10 note. But if he's doing the same thing five days a week for a living and getting utterly browned off then he *will* expect to be paid.

I believe that we have got to see work as something valuable which isn't only linked to remuneration. If a woman's cleaning a house or I'm writing a speech for the House of Lords we don't get paid for it — but it's still work. Yet what people see as giving us status is to go out to work and get paid for it.

If you ask a man, 'What do you do?' he might say, 'I'm a fitter' — and he'll hold his head up and look you straight in the eye. Or he might say, 'I'm unemployed' — but then he'll say it shamefacedly. If you ask a woman, the usual reply is, 'I'm just a housewife. . .' and that means, 'I don't get paid for what I'm doing, so it doesn't count: I don't get any social status out of it'.

When you start asking a few more questions you discover that these people do all sorts of things, like running old people's drop-in centres or writing poetry or goodness knows what. . . but they don't see those things as 'work', because it isn't paid work.

There are some lovely, satisfying things about work when we get it right. There's responsibility — the fact that we are responsible for something. That's the best thing. Another important thing is choice — but for a man

Lord Murray of Epping Forest

Lord (Len) Murray was General Secretary of the TUC from 1973–84, when he retired to involve himself more deeply in a range of voluntary organizations stretching from the National Children's Home to Crisis at Christmas. Retirement — by which he says he means shifting from paid to unpaid work — has given him and his wife Heather more time to do things together in the voluntary field and to catch up with music, opera and theatre.

working on a car assembly line in Dagenham there isn't very much choice about what he does, and perhaps not much responsibility either.

Then for many people there's companionship, and it is at work that they find their friendships and enjoy seeing their mates. There's status: 'He's a doctor', or 'He's a refuse collector. . .' or 'She's a this and he's a that. . .' There is this whole bundle of satisfactions which come from having a job — and also from 'working' (when we get the right definition for work).

Because if you take the fellow who's lying under the car on Saturday morning it's the same sort of thing. He's got the satisfaction of coming out and hearing that the tappets are working. He took the responsibility for doing that — and he's achieved it.

* * *

'For the kingdom of heaven is like a householder who went out early in the morning to hire labourers for his vineyard. After agreeing with the labourers for a denarius a day, he sent them into his vineyard. And going out about the third hour he saw others standing idle in the market place; and to them he said, "You go into the vineyard too, and whatever is right I will give you." So they went.

'Going out again about the sixth hour and the ninth hour, he did the same. And about the eleventh hour he went out and found others standing; and he said to them, "Why do you stand here idle all day?" They said to him, "Because no one has hired us." He said to them, "You go into the vineyard too." '

(Matthew 20:1–7)

A MEDITATION* Sit still for a moment and think about all the things that you are going to do today. What will you do when you put down this book and get up? What are the things that you have got to do, whether you like it or not? What are the things that you will enjoy doing, and that you are looking forward to? Do you believe that God values the things that you do? The washing up? Filling the car up with petrol and checking the tyres? Making a pot of tea? Watering a plant? Travelling to your job (if you have one)? Visiting a friend?

What would happen to the world if the only things that happened were those to do with paid employment and 'proper jobs'? The *Shorter Oxford Dictionary* defines work first of all as 'Something that is or was done; what a person does or did'.

During today, think about the things that someone else you know will do today: an unemployed person. . . an old person. . . a young mother with a family.

A PRAYER* Lord God, help me to understand what work really is — and to delight in the works of your hands and in the works of my hands. Help me to see other people's work as you see it.

WHAT'S FAIR?

If I had been the Trade Union official, the Secretary of the National Union of Vineyard Workers, I'd have had a devil of a job to persuade those labourers in the vineyard that these other brothers ought to get the same as them. They'd have been pressing me to put a claim in to the employer for extra pay for extra work. I'd have argued with them. I'd have said, 'Look at Charlie. . . you know about Charlie. His wife's not very well and his kids haven't got any shoes. He needs the money, mate.'

They might say to me, 'That's all right. We're not going to say he can't have the money. But you go and ask the gaffer for some extra for us. . .' So I go and do that. But if the employer says to me, 'On your bike', then I have to say to these brothers, 'You're not going to get any more. Next time round we'll try and shove the rate up to one and a half denarius. But look. . . these are members of the Union that you're talking about, and you call them brother. But why do you? It's because they've got some sort of claim on you, isn't it mate. . .?'

In the Trade Union movement we usually start our letters, 'Dear Sir and Bro.', and finish up 'Yours fraternally'. What's in between is quite a different matter!

It wasn't until I came back into the church and saw Christians in action in the East End that I asked myself the very simple question: 'Why do I call this man brother and this woman sister? What sense does it make?' The only point in calling someone brother or sister is that we've got a common father. It's the fact of God's fatherhood which gives us this fraternal relationship. There's no rational explanation for it other than that.

The labourers in the vineyard all got some work, even if it wasn't very much. But we need to look at what we do when people can't work at all. The Old Testament recognizes the need for the tribe or the family to look after their own. A perfectly proper expectation is that if you are capable of working then you will work and make your contribution. But it still recognizes that if you are genuinely not able to work then you still have the same rights and the same claims — if you are an old person or if you are sick, or if you are available for work and you can't get it, like our three million unemployed. Some of them have just left school, and they are there in the market place but they can't get work.

Mind you, even if you accept my argument you are left with a dilemma about the people who are too lazy or too feckless to work and use their talents. There are people like that. There are lazy men — men who will send the wife out to work, and who will draw the supplementary benefit and drink it away even though they've got five or six kids — and they get more that way than if he goes to work. We've got to tackle cases like that, even though they are so marginal and so extreme.

But we've got to start by asking ourselves the basic question: 'Do we think that because we are all the children of God, of one Father, men and women are equal? Or do we think that in spite of that we are inherently unequal?' If our answer is that we are all equal in the eyes of God, how dare we act as if any people can be unequal in the eyes of man, and treated as less than equal, less than fairly!

* * *

'When evening came, the owner of the vineyard said to his steward, "Call the labourers and pay them their wages, beginning with the last, up to the first." And when those hired about the eleventh hour came, each of them received a denarius. Now when the first came, they thought they would receive more; but each of them also received a denarius. And on receiving it they grumbled at the householder, saying, "These last worked only one hour, and you have made them equal to us who have borne the burden of the day and the scorching heat." But he replied to one of them, "Friend, I am doing you no wrong; did you not agree with me for a denarius? Take what belongs to you, and go; I choose to give to this last as I give to you. Am I not allowed to do what I choose with what belongs to me? Or do you begrudge my generosity?" So the last will be first, and the first last.' (Matthew 20:8–16)

A PRAYER* Lord God, it says in the Bible that you are 'the Father of all men, especially those who believe. . .' (Romans 4:11). Show me how to love my brothers and my sisters, and how to show my love in action.

Bishop Peter Selby 5/Friday

BEING FAIR TO PEOPLE

I asked Peter Selby what he meant when he talked about justice to the poor, or about justice to anybody.

I am a parent, and as a parent one of the things that you are constantly up against is the growing perception that your children have about fairness. What is fair and what isn't fair? That brings back memories of what it was like when I was a child. It is how I was, and it is how all of us are. We all have a very strong sense that we ought not to be treated worse than other people. It's about not getting a less good birthday present than your sister or brother — and not getting left out when they have a birthday. It's bad enough to have to get used to the fact that you aren't the only one any more — but at least if you aren't the only one then at least you want to be an equal one.

So you mature — through a concept of being the only one, through a concept of fairness (at least an *equal* one) — on to the realization that actually treating everybody equally isn't treating everybody the same. Because simply to treat everybody the same takes no account of the fact that people are different. Therefore people have different needs from other people, and a different thing is a surprise or a joy to different people. So that to get it right is to treat other people equally but differently. It is to build up different people in a different way, so that you treat each one according to the needs of her or his well-being.

It seems to me that is what we have to try to get to and what I think God *has* got to. It's not about treating us all the same, but about giving a lot better treatment to people whose situation is a lot worse.

Biblical images about justice have a lot to do with biblical imges about peace. They are not simply about the scales of justice being equally balanced — although that thought is there, and judges are ordered not to have unequal scales. But there is also the way in which God is said to judge the cause of the poor and needy, which is clearly a highly preferential, caring, merciful thing to do. So that biblically peace and justice is about 'to each according to her well-being. . .' — and that is the only way to peace.

Treating everybody the same *isn't* treating everybody the same, because people all start from different places. And if you treat them all the same they will end up in different places. Therefore attention to everyone's well-being is the only way to deal with that bit in all of us which still retains our childhood — the demand that we should all be treated fairly.

I believe that when the kind of justice I am talking about is done then something Godlike is being done, and that God is in that process. But then you might ask, 'How is it that the poor have even that which they have taken from them?' and 'How is it that the diseased have the added burden of loneliness and that those with AIDS have the added burden of people's contempt?' I suppose that for believers those sorts of questions will always be there, and I think we need to have a conviction that this particular, poignant mystery will not be solved until the end of the age. God's justice, as well as being something that we see and experience and participate in, is also something that we are still waiting for. But what I do *not* think we are waiting for is to know what the character of that justice will be. That is something that we *do* know.

* * *

Say among the nations, 'Yahweh is king.'
The world is set firm, it cannot be moved.
He will judge the nations with justice.

Let the heavens rejoice and earth be glad!
Let the sea thunder, and all it holds!
Let the countryside exult, and all that is in it,
and all the trees of the forest cry out for joy,

at Yahweh's approach, for he is coming,
coming to judge the earth;
he will judge the world with saving justice,
and the nations with constancy.

(Psalm 96:10–13 NJB)

A PRAYER Set before our hearts and minds, Father, the example of our Lord Jesus Christ, who while he was on earth found his refreshment in doing the will of him who sent him and in finishing his work. When many are coming and going and there is little leisure, help us to remember him who knew neither impatience of spirit nor confusion of work and in the midst of all his labours held communion with thee and even on earth was still in heaven.

Bishop Peter Selby 5/Saturday

A SPACE FOR ME

Salvation and peace (*shalom*) are very closely linked, and in biblical understanding there is a notion of spaciousness — like arriving at a plain

Bishop Peter Selby

Peter Selby is the Bishop of Kingston. He is married to Jan and they have three children. He has written *Look for the Living* and *Liberating God*. He is a theologian and is deeply concerned for social justice. He is on the British Refugee Council and Chairman of their Asylum Steering Committee. His personal interests are music and the theatre.

after a trek through the hills. There is a sense that there will be space. When it says that everybody will be under their own vine and fig tree 'and none shall make them afraid', I do not think it is actually about pride of property as we understand it. It is about space, and spaciousness, and the opportunity to spread your arms and not to feel that your room for manoeuvre is under constant threat. Most wars have been about territory — either about the fact that people feel they haven't got that space, or that their space has been taken from them, or that their space is under threat.

I believe what we are made for is something very expansive. . . We are not made to crowd in on one another uninvited. We are made for closeness and for distance.

A friend of mine used to be a drama student, and he said that when people start off on a stage and there are two of them you notice that they lean towards each other to show how related they are to each other. But if it is going to work theatrically then both people have to possess the whole stage. Otherwise they fall in upon one another and cease to be individual persons.

For me that says something very important about the person and the nation, or the group and the society — that spaciousness is a requirement. My desire for all the people that I have anything to do with is that they should have space.

* * *

It shall come to pass in the latter days that the mountain of the house of the Lord shall be established as the highest of the mountains, and shall be raised up above the hills; and peoples shall flow to it, and many nations shall come, and say: Come, let us go up to the mountain of the Lord, to the house of the God of Jacob, that he may teach us his ways and we may walk in his paths.' For out of Zion shall go forth the law, and the word of the Lord from Jerusalem. He shall judge between many peoples, and shall decide for strong nations afar off; and they shall beat their swords into ploughshares, and their spears into pruning hooks; nation shall not lift up sword against nation, neither shall they learn war any more; but they shall sit every man under his vine and under his fig tree, and none shall make them afraid; for the mouth of the Lord of hosts has spoken. (Micah 4:1–4)

A MEDITATION* Imagine yourself sitting on a bench in the park under a big, leafy tree, looking at the crocuses. An old, smelly tramp comes and sits at the other end. How do you feel? Then imagine that you are the tramp, and that when you arrive at your favourite bench for sleeping on you find a well-dressed person sitting on it. How do you feel? In either situation, what do you think Jesus would have felt and have done?

Week 6

PLANET EARTH

OVER TWENTY YEARS AGO my heart suddenly went cold when I listened to Roger Whittaker singing a song. The words were written by a woman, and it was about the tragedy of what man is doing to the earth. The tune started off and then became discordant, with notes that were off key and out of tune, saying what the words were saying.

> 'Something's going wrong, with the singer and the song,
> And the music isn't gentle any more.
> There's a strange and empty sky, where the wild birds used to fly,
> And I never tasted bitter rain before. . .'

If we are to save our beautiful planet earth then more of us will have to join the people who are already working to save it. The World Wildlife Fund, Greenpeace, the Friends of the Earth, the International Fund for Animal Welfare. . .

THE HURTING WORLD

The Spirit of the Lord God is upon me, because the Lord has anointed me to bring good tidings to the afflicted; he has sent me to bind up the brokenhearted, to proclaim liberty to the captives, and the opening of the prison to those who are bound; to proclaim the year of the Lord's favour. . .

(Isaiah 61:1–2)

All good Jews have a passionate love for their Holy Scriptures. . . Do you remember Topol in *Fiddler on the Roof* — 'If I were a rich man. . .'? All the things that he would have if he was rich, and that his wife would have. . . And yes, he wants one staircase going up and another one coming down just for show — but the best thing of all about being rich would be spending hours and hours in the synagogue talking to the holy men about God. . . and talking about the scriptures. Just as Jesus did when he went up to the Temple at Jerusalem when he was 12, and the wise men were astonished at how much he knew and understood. . .

Jesus understood his own call from God in the symbols and imagery and prophecies of the Jewish scriptures. So when he stood up in the synagogue at the start of his ministry he quoted from the great Jewish prophet Isaiah. 'The Spirit of the Lord God is upon me, because the Lord has anointed me. . .', or Christed me. Jesus the Christ simply means Jesus the anointed one — the one whom God anointed with his Spirit. The purpose of the anointing that Isaiah wrote about is to bring good tidings to people who are afflicted and to bind up people who are brokenhearted.

I suppose the essence of being brokenhearted is to be desperately sad about something. Perhaps we've had the sack, so that we haven't got a job to do any more. Perhaps the person whom we love has gone off with someone else. . . and we're feeling hurt and rejected and in a lot of pain. Perhaps we have got an illness that we dread. Or perhaps someone we love has died and there's an aching empty space in our life.

But if we bring the empty space and the heart that is frightened and hurting into the presence of God something seems to happen. I don't know how, but I know it does. There is a comforting and a mending that goes on inside us, and perfect love somehow casts out our fear.

The thing that is hurting us isn't the end of the world. The world is still there, with all the beautiful things that are in it to look at and love — and other people are in it, for us to be friends with and to laugh with and perhaps to cry with.

There are also all the sad and ugly and fearful things in the world that need to be changed and that want us to hold them in our arms and comfort them. . . a world that is hurting, and that needs us to heal it. Somehow our suffering and pain seem to get us closer to the things and the people in the world that are hurting. And it's the suffering of Jesus that means he can bind up the brokenhearted. . .

A PRAYER Lord Christ, give me some of your Spirit to comfort the places in my heart where I hurt. . .Then give me some more of your Spirit, so that I can comfort other people and creatures who are in pain and hurting.

Canon Peter Challen 6/Monday

A PICTURE OF GOD

When my son was very young he asked if we would give him a picture of God for his birthday. That flummoxed us. But my wife and I talked, and we decided that the only thing for us to do was to buy him a beautiful map of the world. So we brought him a map which had little pictures all over it, to show what the different countries were like in terms of their creatures and culture and architecture. We hung it over his bed, and for several years he was confused between God and the world.

Some people would have accused us of pantheism. But what we were struggling with was what is now called pan-en-theism — the idea that God is perceived and understood in all of his creation. He isn't that creation, but he is the force within it. Also, because he is a loving force, there are elements within the creation which have freedom and responsibility — most particularly the human race. But the freedom which the human race has means that it can use it to abort many of the great purposes of God's covenantal relationship with the creation.

I think that map taught my son something. Today he works in social service, and his greatest gift is enabling other people to become themselves. He isn't much of a churchgoer, but I have great confidence that he knows that if the love of God means anything it is in love of creation, love of every person's place within that creation, and deep respect for each individual.

In an important book called *Towards the Recovery of a Lost Bequest*, Roger Dowley indicates how in the translation from Hebrew to Greek (and then to English) we took out the great communal and material insights embodied in the Hebrew language. The abstract, philosophical Greek language belittled the Hebrew, and made it individualized and spiritualized. That was quite unfair to the original, which was about the communal and material setting in which most life is lived, where the land and houses and structures, and the way we behave publicly, are all every bit as much about our spirituality as any private prayer with God. Somehow we've got to teach people to love the whole earth.

An extract from TOWARDS THE RECOVERY OF A LOST BEQUEST. A Layman's worknotes on the biblical pattern for a just community (Scripture Union):

'*The Creation* Several emphases apparent on the face of the creation story serve to negate any over-spiritualized ideas that the people of God are to devote themselves to other-worldly concerns to the exclusion of concern for this present world and its inhabitants. . . Genesis 2:15 and 1:28 import the responsibility of stewardship and good husbandry of the natural creation. The Garden of Eden presents an idealized model of God's *shalom* (peace) intended for those who live in community in obedience to His plan. Enjoyment and gratitude for the joys of God's creation was always and continues to be a characteristic of Jewish faith. Contrasting world-denying strains in Christian tradition stem from post-biblical asceticism, not from Scripture. Maintenance of a wholesome human environment by resistance to pollution can be seen as a Christian's proper response to Scripture, as much as conservation of wild life.

'Perhaps the most telling reference to the solidarity between man and the natural creation in terms of the "new creation" is in Romans 8:18–23, with its

The Revd Canon Peter Challen

Peter Challen is married to Ruth and they have three adult children: a doctor, a midwife and a social worker. Peter is the Senior Chaplain of the South London Industrial Mission. He has laboured in steel and coal and is a SLOAN Fellow of the London Business School. He has written various articles on industrial mission and on theological and faith auditing. When other means are limited he says that he likes travelling in the mind.

picture, so hard for modern Western imagination to conceive, of the whole creation "craning its neck" (v. 19) in anticipation of final deliverance. . . With an effort modern Christians can visualize some restored paradise of meadows, streams and flowers; but reflection suggests that we should be looking for "new creation" renewal where the dereliction is greatest, among the wasted docklands and the industrial spoil tips.'

* * *

The Lord God took the man and put him in the garden of Eden to till it and keep it. (Genesis 2:15)

'Be fruitful and multiply, and fill the earth and subdue it; and have dominion over the fish of the sea and over the birds of the air and over every living thing that moves upon the earth.' (Genesis 1:28)

I consider that the sufferings of this present time are not worth comparing with the glory that is to be revealed to us. For the creation waits with eager longing for the revealing of the sons of God; for the creation was subjected to futility, not of its own will but by the will of him who subjected it in hope; because the creation itself will be set free from its bondage to decay and obtain the glorious liberty of the children of God. We know that the whole creation has been groaning in travail together until now; and not only the creation, but we ourselves, who have the first fruits of the Spirit, groan inwardly as we wait for adoption as sons, the redemption of our bodies.

(Romans 8:18–23)

A PRAYER* Lord God, as we look at this incredible world, may we share some of the joy you know in creating it — and some of your grief as we destroy it. Forgive us. Then give us your Spirit so that we may go out to heal the whole earth instead of hurting it.

Canon Peter Challen 6/Tuesday

THE MANAGEMENT OF PLANET EARTH

Peter Challen had spoken to me about 'planetary management', and I asked him what exactly he meant by it.

The best illustration I can give you was in a recent television programme. It showed two people who purported to come from outer space They were approaching earth from outer space and describing it to each other as if they were seeing it for the first time. What they saw first was its wholeness — all the amazing patterns of colour and cloud. Then as they drew nearer they saw the oceans, and measured the rhythms and cyclical aspects of the creation. As they drew closer and closer they began to be able to observe plant life and water cycles and heat. They had a pretty sophisticated scientific understanding, and they were taking measurements of gas reactions and things like that.

But then they began to discern an animal unlike other animals. First of all they thought that it was made of metal and ran on wheels, although their indicators showed that it had a warm heart. Then one of these animals stopped, and a different sort of being got out. It left the shell of the metal and walked like other animals, except that this one stood upright and walked on two feet. They identified in this creature a source of the imbalance they observed on the earth.

This whole programme showed most beautifully that if you can begin with a devoted, ecstatic view of life then you see the whole thing and you see it whole. You see the planet as one earth and then, within that one earth, you begin to identify what the responsibilities are that have to be taken. You see the way we are to behave in relation to the gases, the water cycles, the heat and the cold, and everything that lives on the face of the earth.

What I mean by planetary management is that we have to play our part in managing it. Our own abilities and position and responsibilities are limited, but with the help of the great traditions and stories — religious, scientific and historical — we can perceive the rich wholeness of the planet from where we are. Then we can do what has to be done from the place where we are.

One of the great insights of our faith is that in the loving creation humanity has been given a peculiar responsibility to have dominion over the whole earth. Human beings are to bear responsibility in stewardship for the maintenance of this enormously delicate, interactive, total planet.

The churches have very quickly got to learn the language of new science, which is summed up in the word 'Gaia'. Gaia represents the concept that the whole earth is a very delicate, interactive, self-sustaining system, which will go beyond a point of recovery if we in our freedom distort and destroy too much.

If we are to take the right path we must identify and use appropriate tools, which will help each one of us to see a vision of life — the life of the planet — and to hold that vision in our own little minds in such a way that we can identify our responsibility. What action should we take? How can we talk with people whose action will be different?

I can give you a precise example of a tool that I have identified. For several years I have been using the *Gaia Atlas of Planet Management*. Within 300 pages there is an amazing picture drawn together by 35 scientists. They took five years to do the work and prepared it as a geography lesson for 4th, 5th or 6th forms. It is no more complicated than that. Yet it is very profound in terms of looking at land and oceans and evolution and civilizations and the other great categories of life on earth.

Once we have grasped the *Gaia Atlas* we have got a way of making a connection with far more people. If we meet someone whose prime responsibility is in relation to work on the land, or on the oceans, we can say to that person, 'What are you doing about the potential of that area of life in which you are working? How do you observe the crisis by your responsibilities? What little bits of renewed insight about management could you practise to divert the terrible crises and recover some of the territory?'

That sort of tool is just what we need. It is written entirely in secular language, but it is suffused with biblical insight of a very exciting kind. Many of the writers are Christians, but they are not needing to proclaim that in specific religious language because they are expressing it in terms of stewardship and an understanding of planet management. Another book is the one I mentioned earlier, *Towards the Recovery of a Lost Bequest*, because that is an extensive examination of biblical scholarship. It shows how we have lost insights about the corporate and the global in our preoccupation with our individuality and our deep psychological needs.

* * *

God made the two great lights: the greater light to govern the day, the smaller light to govern the night, and the stars. God set them in the vault of heaven to shine on the earth, to govern the day and the night and to divide light from darkness. God saw that it was good. Evening came and morning came: the fourth day.

God said, 'Let the waters be alive with a swarm of living creatures, and let birds wing their way above the earth across the vault of heaven.' And so it was. God created great sea-monsters and all the creatures that glide and teem in the waters in their own species, and winged birds in their own species. God saw that it was good. God blessed them, saying, 'Be fruitful, multiply, and fill the waters of the seas; and let the birds multiply on land.' Evening came and morning came: the fifth day.

God said, 'Let the earth produce every kind of living creature in its own species: cattle, creeping things and wild animals of all kinds.' And so it was. God made wild animals in their own species, and cattle in theirs, and every creature that crawls along the earth in its own species. God saw that it was good.

God said, 'Let us make man in our own image, in the likeness of ourselves, and let them be masters of the fish of the sea, the birds of heaven, the cattle, all the wild animals and all the creatures that creep along the ground.'

God created man in the image of himself, in the image of God he created him, male and female he created them. (Genesis 1:16–27 NJB)

A WAY TO PRAY*

Start off by praying. . . Lord God, you have given us dominion over the whole earth. Show us how to love the whole earth and to look after it. Help us to find out what to do.

Then put that prayer in your heart and mind like a seed, so that in the coming weeks and years it will grow into a tree, like the mustard seed in the parable of Jesus.

'With what can we compare the kingdom of God, or what parable shall we use for it? It is like a grain of mustard seed, which, when sown upon the ground, is the smallest of all the seeds on earth; yet when it is sown it grows up and becomes the greatest of all shrubs, and puts forth large branches, so that the birds of the air can make nests in its shade.' (Mark 4:30–32)

Bishop Hugh Montefiore 6/Wednesday

THE RAPE OF THE EARTH

I have been concerned about what is happening to this earth ever since I was an assistant curate. I was up in Newcastle, and there was a marvellous schoolmaster there who wrote a book called *The Estate of Man*. It was that book which first alerted me to the fact that the earth was being raped.

Ever since then I have been much concerned about this whole area. I was the first person to collect together all the facts about what is happening in the world. I wrote a book called *The Question Mark*, and I did it by putting together masses of little cuttings from papers.

One of the ways we are raping the earth is that we are mucking around with it with all our waste processes. It isn't just the way we dispose of our nuclear waste. There are other poisons being dumped on the earth as well, and there are lots of other waste tips.

Another way we are raping the earth is that we are overusing it. There is a maximum use of the earth and there is an optimum use of the earth. At the moment we get as much out of it as we possibly can.

We use fertilisers in order to stimulate it — just as you might take a drug in order to stimulate yourself into being more energetic. But if you take drugs like that you may be very, very energetic for a time, but it doesn't do you any good in the end.

It is the same with the earth. The humus is the living crust on top of the earth — the really rich part of the earth. We are over-stimulating it, and as a result of that its quality is deteriorating and it is disappearing.

The Right Revd Hugh Montefiore

Hugh Montefiore and his wife Elizabeth have 3 daughters and 5 grandchildren. In Cambridge he was first a don then Vicar of Great St Mary's; after that Bishop of Kingston then of Birmingham. He is interested in all God's world, especially in our interpretation of it (theology) and human behaviour (social responsibility and ethics). Books: *Can Man Survive?*; *Jesus Across the Centuries*; *Paul the Apostle*; *The Probability of God*; etc.

We are raping the earth by removing things which are absolutely crucial for our well-being, like trees. Trees have a great effect on climate, and because of that they have an effect on the soil and on the amount of water in the soil.

Another way we are upsetting the balance of nature is to drain marshlands. When we've drained them we think to ourselves, 'How marvellous — now we've got more soil. . .' But the balance of nature requires that there should be wet lands as well as the dry earth.

We are literally removing from the earth at a profligate rate its non-renewable resources like oil. There won't be any oil for our great grandchildren. At least, not very much. It will be terribly expensive.

We are doing the same thing with metals. Some can be re-used, but not all of them.

We cannot necessarily renew our atmosphere as we would wish to do so. The whole balance of nature which cleanses it is not fully in our grasp. It is heating up. We forget too that the vast majority of our planet is full of the sea, and the sea contains very important trace elements which circulate through nature and are necessary for the well-being of life. Now that gets interfered with as well as being polluted.

Those are some of the ways in which the earth is being raped, and by raped I mean violently forced against its will. That is why I use the word. It is not a word that I use lightly.

* * *

'But now, now — it is Yahweh who speaks —
come back to me with all your heart,
fasting, weeping, mourning.'
Let your hearts be broken, not your garments torn,
turn to Yahweh your God again,
for he is all tenderness and compassion,
slow to anger, rich in graciousness,
and ready to relent. . .
O soil, do not be afraid;
be glad, rejoice,
for Yahweh has done great things.
Beasts of the field, do not be afraid;
the pastures on the heath are green again,
the trees bear fruit,
vine and fig tree yield abundantly.

(Joel 2:12–13, 21–22 JB)

STUDY GROUP MATERIAL

Planet Earth

1. Begin with the Coventry Cathedral Prayer.

2. Perhaps read out Hugh Montefiore's interview for Friday. Do you really believe it is happening as people say, or do you think you are being like an ostrich and burying your head in the sand?

3. Read out the extract from *Towards the Recovery of a Lost Bequest* in Monday's interview. Then read out the last paragraph of Peter Challen's interview that day. Discuss what they say.

PRAYING Sit still and in silence for a few minutes. Then read out the extract from Revelation 8 and 9 at the end of Hugh Montefiore's Thursday interview. Stay silent for a few more minutes, and see the pictures in your mind. Then perhaps share some of your feelings with one another.

Finish by reading out the prayer by Dostoevsky at the end of Hugh Montefiore's first interview on Wednesday.

A PRAYER Lord, may we love all your creation, all the earth and every grain of sand in it. May we love every leaf, every ray of your light. May we love the animals: you have given them the rudiments of thought and joy untroubled. Let us not trouble them; let us not harass them, let us not deprive them of your happiness, let us not work against your intent. For we acknowledge unto you that all is like an ocean, all is flowing and blending, and that to withhold any measure of love from anything in your universe is to withhold that same measure from you.

(Feodor Dostoevsky, adapted from *The Brothers Karamazov*)

Bishop Hugh Montefiore 6/Thursday

ON BEHALF OF POSTERITY

When I realized that nature was being raped I thought that there were some things which had to be done. One was that Christians themselves should be alerted to the situation.

It is not often realized that Christians have a very bad reputation for conservation and ecology. I was so concerned about this area that when I was on the Doctrine Commission I persuaded the Archbishop of Canterbury, Dr Ramsey, to set up a small group of us to look at the theology of nature. We produced our report, *Man and Nature*, and I remember that Max Nicholson, the head of the Nature Conservancy, came down to talk to us. He accused Christians of being the major cause of the rape of nature.

I think that was a bit unfair. But there is no doubt that theology does come into this. Because if you think that nature is fallen, and if you think of the external world as being no good at all (and that it is only spiritual things that matter) then you can do what you like with it. I think it is fair to say that this is how Calvinism looked on nature, and that sort of attitude encouraged the business man to make what profits he could out of the natural world without taking any thought for the effects it would have.

But in those days it was all on a much smaller scale. The problem has arisen now because of the vast scale in which we get at nature and pollute it — or prevent it from blossoming in the way that it should do. It is the scale that matters, and the scale is such that ecology is now no longer a national issue. It is an international issue.

The acid from our factory chimneys goes over the North Sea and makes the Swedish and Norwegian lakes infertile. That's international. But it isn't only happening there. It's happening here.

I once appeared at an enquiry in Wales when they wanted to make a reservoir to produce a lot more water for Swansea. They asked me, 'Who are you appearing for?' I said, 'I am appearing for posterity' — and they had to write that down as though Posterity was a man. They wanted water because they had no industrial re-use and they had a tremendous leakage problem. We suggested a much better place where they could have a reservoir, but they stuck to their plan of having a piece of marvellous natural country, where there were *lizards*! They flooded it and made an artificial lake.

But they said, 'We won't upset the fishing. There's a lot of money in fishing'. So they made a salmon trap so that they could cart the salmon from one side of the lake to the other to go on up to spawn. But they needn't have bothered. The acid rain is such that there aren't any fish now in that part of Wales.

That has taken about ten years. It has happened largely through the Forestry Commission and through people endowing their children by planting pine trees. This is a typical way in which ecology gets upset. There are tremendous inducements for the wealthy to buy up land and plant it with pine trees. Pine trees take quite a short time to grow and there are all kinds of tax remissions and tax allowances for looking after the forest. Then later on their children can get thousands and thousands of pounds when the pine trees are cut down.

That sounds admirable, because we have very few forests in this country. But when you plant a lot of forests like that you upset the ecology and get a lot of acidity in the soil. It gets into the rain, and wherever enough acid rain falls things start to die.

The Friends of the Earth say that it seems likely that in this country we have about four years before anything really drastic happens. The extraordinary thing about the Black Forest in Germany is that once it started, it happened so quickly. It starts in a very small way but it escalates. First of all you see dead leaves at the wrong time of year. Then you see dead branches. Gradually you see the whole tree dying, with only a few branches alive.

The pictures I have seen of these dead forests are terrible. Trees need a tremendous amount of water. They take it up from the earth, and if the water is polluted it upsets the whole balance of their economy inside.

* * *

When the Lamb opened the seventh seal, there was silence in heaven for about half an hour. Then I saw the seven angels who stand before God, and seven trumpets were given to them. . . The first angel blew his trumpet, and there followed hail and fire, mixed with blood, which fell on the earth; and a third of the earth was burnt up, and a third of the trees were burnt up, and all green grass was burnt up.

The second angel blew his trumpet, and something like a great mountain, burning with fire, was thrown into the sea; and a third of the sea became blood, a third of the living creatures in the sea died, and a third of the ships were destroyed.

The third angel blew his trumpet, and a great star fell from heaven, blazing like a torch, and it fell on a third of the rivers and on the fountains of water. The name of the star is Wormwood. A third of the waters became wormwood, and many men died of the water, because it was made bitter. . .

The rest of mankind, who were not killed by these plagues, did not repent of the works of their hands nor give up worshipping demons and idols of gold and silver and bronze and stone and wood, which cannot either see or hear or walk; nor did they repent of their murders or their sorceries or their immorality or their thefts. (Revelation 8:1–11; 9:20–21)

A PRAYER Lord God, you are our father and our mother. You have formed us out of the dust of the earth. Help us to love and honour the earth as we do you. (Barbara Wood)

Bishop Hugh Montefiore 6/Friday

THE RICHNESS OF CREATION

But look at Behemoth, my creature, just as you are!
  He feeds on greenstuff like the ox,
but what strength he has in his loins,
  what power in his stomach muscles!
His tail is as stiff as a cedar,
  the sinews of his thighs are tightly knit.
His bones are bronze tubes,
  his frame, like forged iron.
He is the first of the works of God.
  His Maker threatened him with the sword,
forbidding him the mountain regions
  and all the wild animals that play there.
Under the lotus he lies,
  he hides among the reeds in the swamps.
The leaves of the lotus give him shade,
  the willows by the stream shelter him.
(Job 40:15–22 NJB)

I believe that God takes great pleasure in the richness and variety of his creation. God has initiated the process, and he undergirds it with his power.

He has supported this almost unimaginable process of evolution, taking place over millions of years, with all the species coming into existence as a result of slight genetic alterations and different habitats and different environments.

Sometimes we human beings imagine that God only takes delight in us. My own view is that we must give him a lot of sadness — whereas the other species haven't got free will, and he must take great pleasure in their beauty and their variety, and in their wonderful intricacy and the way they have evolved.

Human beings are created to be stewards of all this. In the wonderful story tale of Genesis man is there to be the gardener. He is meant to look after all these species — not to kill them and put them out of the way. That seems to be a very important aspect of what man ought to do and what he doesn't do.

I love that picture of man being the gardener. But Genesis says that the gardener disobeyed and so was thrown out of the garden. Now, in forgiveness and redemption, how could a redeemed gardener garden on this earth?

We would properly conserve things, to see that species didn't die out. We would seek to prevent disasters — the sort of disasters that are caused by acid rain and by other kinds of pollution. We would do it by taking precautions, and by being moderate in the use that we make of resources. I don't mean that we would starve ourselves, but we could be moderate. If we all drive very fast we are using up vast quantities of non-renewable oil — so we would drive more slowly. If we act temperately we can do it.

Then we should join a pressure group which is concerned with conserving nature. It is the structures which need to be changed. The law needs to be altered, because human beings are naturally greedy. We don't naturally think of future generations. So we need laws which restrain us, and if we are going to have new laws then we need pressure groups.

That is one of the reasons why I am particularly concerned with the Friends of the Earth. I have also been on the World Wildlife Appeal Council, to get millions and millions of pounds in order to keep proper nature reserves. One of the really encouraging things is that there is a lot of good will. Vast sums of money have been given, just as large numbers of ordinary people join these pressure groups. So I am not without hope that the world is beginning to wake up just in time. But it will be a very close thing to put things right.

Do you find any conflict in yourself between millions of pounds going towards preserving animal species when there are millions of human beings dying of hunger?

There is a conflict. There is bound to be. I think it is a conflict which bears most hardly on the Third World. The response of the Third World to conservation is largely, 'You, the rich world! You have drained us of resources! You have made yourselves rich on our raw materials! And now you wish us to stop, while we remain poor.' There is some truth in this argument and that is why I have talked about this country rather than other countries. I don't think we ought to try to prevent people from using resources, only from using them all up.

One matter I have been concerned with is the rain forests, because we have been concerned with that in the Friends of the Earth. It is possible to introduce cutting programmes which involve replanting, so that you are not actually ruining the soil under the rain forest. It is very poor soil and when stripped of trees the only thing it is any good for is to produce the cheapest quality beef which is made into hamburgers for fast food.

It is a horrible thought, but many people who eat hamburgers are in fact eating the scraggy cattle which once grazed where the rain forests were. But it is possible to introduce programmes which involve replanting. And these countries do need hard currency, so they need to sell the wood to people who make furniture in Europe and in the West.

A WAY TO PRAY The richness of God's world is a way that we can worship the creator through the created. We can see something of the glory of God by looking at his handiwork. We can be inspired by the glory of God and his richness through sitting and looking at a funny thing like a spider — and looking at all sorts of different animals. This can be almost a meditation.

We can put ourselves in perspective so far as God is concerned by realizing that he has other interests besides ourselves. We can learn that by looking at nature and reflecting on it. As we go on reflecting on these things we shall become aware of the bounty of nature. The extraordinary thing about the natural order is its generosity, and the fecundity of its reproductive power. So we can learn from it about the generosity of God — and also the vast amount of waste he is prepared to countenance in order to gain his ends.

A PRAYER **King's Son**

Lord,
isn't your creation wasteful?
Fruits never equal
the seedlings' abundance.
Springs scatter water.
The sun gives out
enormous light.
May your bounty teach me
greatness of heart.
May your magnificence
stop me being mean.
Seeing you a prodigal
and open-handed giver,
let me give unstintingly
like a king's son,
like God's own.

(Archbishop Helder Camara)

NO MAN IS AN ISLAND

As I have written in *Liberating God*, I am absolutely clear that all personal disturbance is a reflection of the invasion of the world's disturbance into the lives of persons. My feelings and my behaviour are the result of some inner encounter between me and the world around me, so that in part I do for others what they are unwilling to do for themselves. And they do for me in return much of what I am unwilling to do for myself.

This close intertwining of human lives is most beautifully expressed by Kahil Gibran when the prophet is asked to speak about crime and punishment:

'Oftentimes have I heard you speak of those who commit a wrong as though they were not part of you, but strangers unto you and intruders upon your world.
But I say that even as the holy and the righteous cannot rise beyond the highest which is in each one of you,
So the wicked and the weak cannot fall lower than the lowest which is in you also.
And as a single leaf turns not yellow but with the silent knowledge of the whole tree,
So the wrongdoer cannot do wrong without the hidden will of you all. . .

'If any of you would bring to judgement the unfaithful wife,
Let him also weigh the heart of her husband in scales and measure his soul with measurements.
And let him who would lash the offender look unto the spirit of the offended.
And if any of you would punish in the name of righteousness and lay the axe unto the evil tree, let him see to its roots;
And verily he will find the roots of the good and the bad, the fruitful and the fruitless, all entwined together in the silent heart of the earth.'

One of the things that comes out of group dynamics is the whole notion of projection. When somebody acts out really angrily, the place of discovery and learning is when people get to the point of saying, 'That anger was also mine. I didn't recognize it at the time, and I didn't feel it at the time — but now I see it.'

The sort of politics I detest just writes off people as though they were not of us. If we are talking about 'the unemployed', we mustn't do it in a way which implies that the fact of their unemployment (and their 'laziness') is theirs and not ours.

Simon Phipps told a marvellous story of a plane which had crashed under the sea, and the passengers were still in it and still alive, under the water. A crew member said he would go up through the water with a dinghy and try to raise the alarm, and a passenger said, 'I'll go with you because I'm a skin diver'. But the passenger's wife was furious. He said, 'Why are you furious, it'll be for the good of all of us. . .' But the wife said 'Us! You and I are us. . . This is just a lot of strangers.' And the sermon was about 'If God be for us, who can be against us?' It was brilliant, and I think it was about that intertwining of our lives that I am talking about.

* * *

'Judge not, that you be not judged. For with the judgement you pronounce you will be judged, and the measure you give will be the measure you get. Why do you see the speck that is in your brother's eye, but do not notice the log that is in your own eye? Or how can you say to your brother, "Let me take the speck out of your eye," when there is the log in your own eye? You hypocrite, first take the log out of your own eye, and then you will see clearly to take the speck out of your brother's eye.' (Matthew 7:1–5)

A MEDITATION* Hold in your mind the person or the group in society whom you find yourself the most condemning towards. Then re-read that extract from *The Prophet*. After that, hold yourself and them in the light of God, and just stay there for a few moments.

(Editor) Sunday

GOD WITH US

He was despised and rejected by men; a man of sorrows, and acquainted with grief; and as one from whom men hide their faces he was despised, and we esteemed him not. Surely he has borne our griefs and carried our sorrows; yet we esteemed him stricken, smitten by God, and afflicted. But he was wounded for our transgressions, he was bruised for our iniquities; upon him was the chastisement that made us whole, and with his stripes we are healed. All we like sheep have gone astray; we have turned every one to his own way; and the Lord has laid on him the iniquity of us all. . . (Isaiah 53:3–6)

Today's reading is a success story. But it's a very odd one, because the success was born out of total failure. It's about someone who succeeds in doing what he's after and what God's after. Isaiah says that he's the servant of God. 'Behold, my servant shall prosper. . . he shall be exalted and lifted up, and shall be very high. . .'

But it's a strange way of prospering, and when people look at him they don't always see it. 'As many were astonished at him — his appearance was so marred, beyond human semblance, and his form beyond that of the sons of men. . .' They see a man nailed on to a wooden cross, twisting his body in agony because of the pain. . .

A doctor I know tells a story about a man who was sent to prison for committing robbery with violence. When he was in prison he started to believe in God. Then he became a Christian, and someone gave him a little wooden crucifix that he used to keep in his pocket.

Sometimes the violence that was still inside him used to erupt like a volcano. But he didn't let it out on the other prisoners. Instead, what he would do was to clench his fist round the crucifix and let all his fury and hatred and anger pour into that. Sometimes he broke the cross with its figure of Christ nailed on to it, and then he had to send out for another one. . .

It's strange how much evil that man on the cross can absorb into himself— like a great sponge mopping up the world's sin. . . 'We have done those things which we ought not to have done, and we have left undone those things which we ought to have done. . .' And to add to that sometimes we're sad and we're disappointed and we're desolate — and we can bring those things along as well: 'surely he has borne our griefs, and carried our sorrows. . .'

And it works for us because of his desolation. When we are feeling despised and rejected we are not going to relate very well to some triumphalist figure who has had roses all the way and hasn't got the remotest idea what it's like to be us. That sort of person can't do anything for us at all.

But 'a man of sorrows, and acquainted with grief. . .' — he can do something for us, and we can relate to that. And to someone who cried out from the cross, 'My God, my God, why have you forsaken me. . .?'

Yet it says that 'God was in Christ, reconciling the world to himself, and not counting their trespasses against them. . .' But we need to see it happening — in a man dying in great pain on a cross outside Jerusalem. . .

If thou, O God, the Christ didst leave,
In him, not thee, I do believe;
To Jesus dying all alone
To his dark Cross, not thy bright Throne,
My hopeless hands will cleave.

But if it was thy love that died,
Thy voice that in the darkness cried,
The print of nails I long to see,
In thy hands, God, who fashioned me.
Show me *thy* pierced side. (author unknown)